D1483585

An African Student in China

An African Student in China

Emmanuel John Hevi

FREDERICK A. PRAEGER, *Publisher*

NEW YORK · LONDON

FREDERICK A. PRAEGER, *Publisher*
64 University Place, New York 3, N.Y., U.S.A.
77-79 Charlotte Street, London W.1, England

Published in the United States of America in 1963
by Frederick A. Praeger, Inc., Publisher

Printed in Great Britain

TO MOTHER AFRICA

Contents

Introduction

This book is a record of my experiences in China and, in part also, in the Soviet Union and North Korea. I intend it mainly for Africans.

It is not an academic treatise; for academic treatises I have no qualification. My sole qualification for writing it is that I have been to places you have not been to; seen, heard and experienced things you have not.

But it is not a mere traveller's tale either. It is an argument: my argument against communism in Africa.

I have a fourfold purpose in writing it:

First, to tell Africa what Communist China is really like.

I am aware that China's propaganda services beam daily radio broadcasts to Africa in English, French, Arabic, Swahili and possibly other African languages. I know also that vast quantities of their magazines and periodicals reach Africa. Since I know the Chinese communists for the inveterate liars they are, I do not expect them to cease trying to persuade us that China is a paradise and that communism is the one and only possible road to such a paradise. I have been the target of such false propaganda, and I am all too well aware of its effects on persons who have no alternative and reliable sources of information. My account is meant as a counterblast to the falsehoods you have heard about China in the past and are likely to hear in the future.

Secondly, to make Africa realise the direction in which President Nkrumah of Ghana is moving and to warn that, given the right opportunity, he will lead all Africa along the road he believes in—the road to the Chinese brand of socialism I saw.

Even China's best friends of recent memory, the Soviet Union and almost all other communist countries, now condemn China's aggressiveness, now mock at China for her great flops. But when Ghana's President looked far and near and all around, he found no other country he could copy but this very China.

Nkrumah has succeeded in outwitting people like that young Ghanaian who, after touring China in December 1960, declared to me in Peking and in the presence of other witnesses: 'Anyone who brings this kind of socialism to Ghana will find himself in the gutter the next day.' That man returned to Ghana and saw 'this kind of socialism' introduced into his country step by step. He was impotent to act. His hands had already been tied and his mouth gagged by preventive detention laws and other and equally vicious laws. Look around Africa, and you will find at least one country closely following in Ghana's footsteps. *Your* country may be next.

Thirdly, to guide and warn African students intending to study in China.

For a long time we have been modelled by Western ideas, and an African student going to Britain, France or America, or even to such communist countries as Poland and Czechoslovakia, meets with many of the same essentially Western ways and *mores*. But China is in the Far East. For centuries of her civilised history she has been isolated from the rest of the world and her brief contacts with Western civilisations have changed little in her essentially Eastern ways and *mores*. A student from Africa therefore enters an almost completely new world the moment he crosses the Chinese frontier. Add to this the fact that China is communist: the most fanatically communist country in the world today. Any African student will be lost, just as those who packed up and left Peking in 1962, dissatisfied and disgusted, were lost, if he does not know a little about the realities of that country beforehand. If, knowing something of the realities, he still insists on going, then at least his shock will be less violent than ours. He will at least have known what to expect. We did not. What counts more, the comrades have learned from us pioneers that the African is no longer a savage who may be bullied and bulldozed with impunity.

Fourthly, to demonstrate that the adoption of communism does not in itself cure those ills we would like to get rid of. On the contrary, the introduction of this system often perpetuates those very evils we have most cause to abhor, besides leaving us in many respects much worse than we were before.

*   *   *

In my condemnation of communism, I stand on a different platform from that of the American, the British, the French or any other capitalists. For them I hold no brief.

I belong to no established capitalist system which it is in my interest to protect. Being of a peasant family with no capital or sizeable property to cling to, I lose little of material wealth through the introduction of a communist system.

My stand is based solely and entirely on the conviction that the individual is supreme: his needs take precedence over the mere prestige of the state; and on the realisation that the kind of system I saw practised in

China is an insult at once to the body and mind of a people supposed to be free and sovereign.

This system—based on the principle that an individual may be callously dispossessed of his property or 'justly' murdered or imprisoned without fair trial or arbitrarily deprived of the reasoned exercise of his will, all so that a state may grow great in prestige and a clique of political oligarchs maintain for ever their power over a deceived people—is a system with which I can never agree.

Men seek happiness; men seek contentment. Some interpret happiness and contentment in terms of gold, others in terms of service to their fellow men, and yet others in terms of tasks well fulfilled.

I believe that all men should have the right to order their lives according to their own beliefs, always providing they give due respect to the just laws of the land and the rights of their fellow men.

Man has never been satisfied with nature as he found it. God gave man two legs: he built wheels and rolled, built himself wings and flew. Still not content with these and many other wonderful achievements, man would change his very nature. But how far can we go? Can we change all men's nature to make all men conform to one pattern? I do not believe so. Even identical twins do not think alike or act exactly alike. What sense is there in demanding that men born of different parents, bred in different environments, given different education, men all with their own spark of individuality in them, should all think alike, act alike?

*   *   *

More than a year has elapsed since my return from the communist countries, and this absolves me somewhat from the charge often levelled at students: the charge of seeking publicity. But I shall heartily welcome and accept as compliments such endearing communist epithets as 'bourgeois reactionary', 'subversive element', 'imperialist 'lackey' and so forth, which the Eastern comrades and their friends in Africa will certainly hurl at me when they find themselves at a loss for better argument.

In saying, 'we Africans' throughout this work, I am not in any way assuming a role outside my competence. I say it in exactly the same spirit that prompts every true African nationalist to regard Tshombe, Welensky, Verwoerd and Salazar as a personal enemy; that spirit which moves an East African to protest against French atom tests in North Africa, or a West African to cry death to the Portuguese murderers in Angola.

In all these and many more, every African owes a duty to Mother Africa.

July 1963.   E. John Hevi

PART I

The China I Saw

1

First Impression

My first contact with the People's Republic of China took place when the poorly heated and poorly pressurised Ilushin plane which took us from Rangoon *via* Mandalay touched down in the provincial capital, Kunming. We arrived at about 3 o'clock on November 27, 1960. We had departed from Accra seven days earlier, three student companions and I, and travelled through Lagos, Kano, Khartoum, Beirut, and Rangoon, and were received at Kunming airport by two broadly smiling Chinese comrades, one representing the All-China Federation of Trade Unions, which had granted us scholarships, and the other representing the Chinese Tourist Agency. The hotel they took us to was quite presentable and the city itself (that is to say the parts of it that I saw) was clean and appeared well planned.

But it was neither the city itself nor the red-scarved youth pioneers that struck me at first—it was the inhabitants. To be more precise, it was their attitude, not towards us poor travellers, but towards life in general. Upon seeing them a vivid picture leaped into my mind— the picture of a poor little dog in the presence of a big hostile dog of vastly superior strength. Imagine such a weakling dog, tail between hind legs, body half-flexed as if about to crouch in supplication, piteous and frightened eyes watching intently every move of the burly aggressor. Every single muscle in the little dog's puny body is tuned to show utter resignation and submission to superior power. The general attitude of the people of Kunming and, as I discovered later, of the whole of China, was an exact representation of the attitude of that puppy. They went about with down-cast eyes and with a furtive manner as if resigned to a fate they were powerless to alter. They were fearful of something. I did not know then, but I know now, that this 'something' is the Chinese Communist Party.

The Chinese have a popular song which begins:

> Shè hùi zhǔ yì hǎo, shè hùi zhǔ yì hǎo,
> Shè hùi zhǔ yì guó jiā rén mín dì wèi gāo
> Fǎn dòng pài bèi dǎ dǎo
> Dì guó zhǔ yì jiā zhě wěi bǎ táo pǎo lě.

In English that means:

> Socialism is good, Socialism is good,
> The people of socialist countries occupy an exalted
>   position;
> Reactionaries have been overthrown,
> Imperialism is fleeing with tail between its legs.

A very good point indeed, that about imperialism; and I also, the ardent anti-imperialist that I am, do wish with all my heart that all imperialists would flee to damnation with their tails tight between their hind legs. But, looking back, I think that the part of their song which tells of imperialism fleeing with its tail between its legs more fittingly describes the rank and file of the Chinese people themselves—the masses, that powerless and resigned section of the population which can be bullied and whose legs can be pulled in any direction. And those who do the bullying and the leg-pulling are the Chinese communist bosses. Enlightenment did not come to me all of a sudden at the time I saw the look of dejection and the attitude of resignation of the Kunming people; enlightenment came by slow degrees during the one-and-a-half years of my stay in China. And God forbid that the people of any part of Africa should ever have to suffer the abject humiliation which is now the lot of the masses in China.

'Comparisons are odious', they say, and I've no doubt that those who don't like what they read here will try to dismiss its relevance in some such way as the ambassador of an African state who tried to dissuade me from a particular type of comparison by quoting the African adage: 'It is comparison that disgraces the ass.' I'm not quite sure if this means whether it is the comparer who is an ass, or whether it is a question of the ass's never knowing he is an ass until someone compares him to an ass. Be that as it may; my point is that the Chinese people—human beings like all of us, a people with a great history of human achievement—have been reduced by fear of communist tyranny to the status of weak animals brutally tamed by 'boss' animals.

The day following our arrival in Kunming, we continued our journey by the same plane to Peking, capital of the People's Republic of China. Here also there was a reception committee awaiting us, this time a very imposing affair consisting of two officials of the All-China Federation of Labour, and the dean of the Foreign Students' Department and other staff of the Institute of Foreign Languages, together with an interpreter. We were received with all the outward signs of cordiality. After very casual immigration and customs formalities, we were taken, with hugs, hand-shakes and back-slaps, to a sumptuous banquet in the airport's restaurant. There were many speeches and toasts to the eternal friendship of the African and the Chinese peoples.

The banquet over, we boarded an ancient and rickety bus which loudly proclaimed its age in the many creaking noises it made as it trundled along. That drive to the Institute seemed to last an eternity. Despite our woollen clothes, we found the weather bitterly cold, and to us who had lived all our lives around the Equator, it was veritable torture to be suddenly transplanted into that piercingly cold climate. As I sat shivering with cold, I could not help speculating on exactly which of the two, our bus or a tortoise, would win a mile race. That bus was just too slow!

Half-frozen, we finally reached the Western Compound of the Institute of Foreign Languages just as the Chinese students, their evening studies finished, were trooping back to their dormitories in the Eastern Compound. The hand-claps which greeted us at the gate would ordinarily have warmed our hearts, but we were too chilled to the marrow to linger in reciprocating them. Our one concern was to get to a warm place. At long last, we reached our dormitories and were tucked in, suit, shoes and all, under warm quilts. Slowly the circulation returned to our fingers, toes, nose-tips and ears, and we became our former selves, able once more to chatter away with our Chinese interpreters and with African students who had arrived in China ahead of our party.

That first night I lay awake a long time, turning over memories of the events that led me to China, of my wife and family, my parents and relatives, of all the friends I had left behind me thousands of miles away. And I thought of the seven years of hard work that lay ahead before I could qualify as a doctor. The warmth of the greeting we had received from the Chinese also held my attention for a long time that night. I noticed then and subsequently how especially cordial was the welcome given to students from Ghana. At first, this pleased and impressed me. It was only later that I came to realise that there were special reasons for this special welcome given to Ghanaians, and that the Chinese reserve their most cordial greetings for people whose countries are known, or expected, to be travelling along the same road as China—to communism.

As time went on, I became more and more uneasy at this singling out of the Ghanaian students for special consideration by the Chinese.

*   *   *

There is something you just cannot fail to notice on your first visit to Peking: almost everybody—men and women, young and old—wears blue clothing. The impression is of a vast army in blue uniform. The only relief from the eternal blue are the scarves or shawls with which the women usually (but by no means always) cover their heads. The men generally wear skull-caps or blue cloth caps or go bareheaded. Often it is only by the headgear that you can tell with any certainty which are the men and which the women, for, since both sexes wear trousers and the same kind of blue overcoat, all of the same coarse cotton cloth, the two sexes look alike as you pass them in the street. In wintertime, the trousers and overcoats consist of two layers of cloth with thick cotton padding in between. This gives everybody a bloated appearance which at first sight can easily be mistaken for fatness. Here and there you meet a soldier of the Liberation Army. The style of the soldier's uniform is exactly the same as that of the general populace, but the colour is khaki instead of blue.

The higher officials of the Party are a class to themselves and their clothes are distinctive albeit still in the ubiquitous blue. Their trousers and tunics, the latter

buttoned up to the chin, are made of good gaberdine.
Cloth of this quality is too expensive for any save the
highly placed to afford. Over this they wear a Western-
style overcoat (again blue), topping it all with a fur cap
which may cost anything between 50 and 200 yuan
(between £7 10s. and £30 approximately; a bus conductor,
for example, earns 18 yuan, about £2 12s. a month).

The marks of femininity and taste which distinguish
women in other countries from their menfolk are almost
entirely lacking in the women of the New China. It
therefore took me some time to sort out the details by
which to recognise who was who. Chinese women
generally have more oval faces with eyes set wider apart
than the men. Most of them wear their hair cut short
and round at the nape of the neck. This style, I understand, is the one approved by the Party. All the attention
it needs is a few passes of the comb and a short tail tied
on one side of the head by a piece of coloured cloth or a
plastic string. Less conformist women wear their hair in
two long plaits dangling down the back or coiled, cockle-
shell fashion, at the back of the head. But all, with hardly
any exception whatever, wear blue.

How do the Chinese explain this eternal blue? They
say that for centuries colour has had a social significance
for the Chinese people. Yellow was the colour of the
emperor, blue the colour of the masses, and there were
various other colours for different gradations of society.
Foreigners often found it difficult to appreciate the social
significance of colour in China. The story is well known
of the English merchant in the mid-nineteenth century
who simply could not understand why he was unable to
sell pins to the Chinese, for he had been told they were in
great demand. It turned out that he was offering the
pins in yellow packets; it would have been *lèse-majesté for*
ordinary Chinese to buy *yellow* packets of pins.

Many things have changed in China since the days of the Celestial Empire, but the colour fetish, far from declining, has been given a new lease of life by the present régime. The Party argues that, since socialist New China is a government of the masses, it is right and proper that everyone should adopt the colour of the masses—blue.

There was no direct attempt, it seems, to force the people to adopt blue, beyond commending its proletarian, democratic significance. But direct compulsion was not necessary. All the textile factories belong to the state, all that was necessary was to ensure that the factories made nothing save blue cloth. The individual was left perfectly free to wear the blue cloth—or go naked. There is no possibility of the masses buying imported cloth, so blue it is.

Why this insistence on uniformity in dress? Communism aims at the elimination of individualism and the eventual regimentation of all aspects of the people's life. This aim is implemented in various forms in communist societies. In China, one form is to secure uniformity of dress. This gradually conditions people to think in terms of the collective rather than of their individual selves. Getting everybody to dress in the approved blue brings the people closer to the collectivism the Party desires to impose.

I have travelled recently in a West African country where I observed that the people are very fond of blue colour for their dress. These people, of their own free will, choose blue as their favourite colour and dress in it to please themselves. No one forced them into blue; no one tried to prevent them from dressing in any other colours should they wish to do so.

One day, perhaps, we of Africa may also go the communist way. Then doubtless an all-powerful and all-pervading party will require us to demonstrate our affiliation or loyalty by wearing clothes of a prescribed colour and style. Gone then will be the gay and multi-coloured clothes that make any African country a place to remember. Gone will be the differences in style and material which lend to every African man and woman a distinctive personality. And gone also will be the ear-rings and necklaces, the bright shoes and coquettish hair-dos and all those other little adornments that make the African woman really look like a woman: a sight to gladden the heart of any man who is a man. When that day comes, we shall dress alike in colour and style; our women will look like dowdy imitations of the men, and that thing called sex-appeal will disappear. Our womenfolk will be dressed exactly like us men, with their hair cut short like a boy's, because there will be no incentive for, and every discouragement against, doing the hair in complicated and beautiful styles. There will be no time for such 'useless' occupations. The Party will see to it that we are all kept busy from dawn to dusk on more 'important' matters. When that day comes, God help Africa!

What I have said about Chinese dress refers particularly to winter-dress. To some extent of late, people have been getting a little bolder as the initial fanaticism of the 'liberation' wears off. In summertime especially, colours other than blue are beginning to appear on the streets. But somehow the idea still persists that people who wear tasteful, neat clothes have 'bourgeois, capitalist' inclina-tions. We foreign students often had such epithets tagged on to us even though, to our minds, the clothes we usually wore out there in China would have been con-sidered rather shabby elsewhere. To the 'correct-thinking' Chinese, the more faded or shapeless one's dress, the more socialist one is (but a fair number of high-ups manage to combine sound socialism with at least good quality, if not colourful, clothing).

Undoubtedly, simplicity in dress is to be expected at a time of austerity and in the early struggles of a nation to get on its feet again, and it can be regarded as meritorious in a people to reject ostentation when going through a period of difficult social reconstruction. But simplicity is one thing; a deliberate policy of drab and shabby uniformity is quite another.

I see no merits in such a policy. Arguments in defence of it are based on exactly the same foundations as those of Mr Fox when the grapes he could not get suddenly became sour grapes. Our brighter, better clothing was 'reactionary' and so forth because the Chinese could not, and their leaders would not let them if they could, obtain them.

I came across many other manifestations of this Chinese 'unattainable-grapes-are-sour' mentality during my stay in their country.

In winter especially, surgical masks form an important part of clothing for the Chinese. They are intended as a hygienic measure: a very wise one indeed in a country where people tend to spit anywhere they happen to be standing—in the street, in cinemas and theatres, and even in the lecture halls of the universities. Professor Sriparti Chandra Sekhar, whose interesting book on Red China I have read since my return home, records that spitting is now rare in China. I don't know enough about the matter to be able to make a firm judgment whether it is rarer now than it used to be, but I certainly observed the habit in pretty general use while I was there. The fact is, I think, that the Chinese, like all human beings, have a knack of slipping back into the old ruts when the pressure that forced them into new ways is released. At the time when Professor Sekhar was in

China, the campaign against spitting and house-flies was at its peak and he saw offenders being severely rebuked. By the time I got there, the pressure had slackened somewhat and the people were relapsing into their old ways.

I remember asking a lady comrade at a banquet: 'Back home I read in a book that you have exterminated all the house-flies in your country. Is it true?' Her answer was: 'Of course there are still some left.' It was winter then and the flies were hibernating. When spring came, the flies came with it, in as great hordes as ever I have seen in my own or any other country. It was little things like this that taught me eventually to look carefully into Chinese claims before accepting them as fact.

Besides the sheer cold, Peking's winter has always got nasty tricks up its sleeve, making the use of surgical masks very necessary. You are walking along the street or about the campus when suddenly, with no warning whatever, a fierce gust of wind whips out at you from the north. It fills your nose, eyes, ears and every vulnerable crevice of your body with brown dust before you know what is happening. It dies down just as suddenly as it came, leaving you coughing and spluttering and with smarting eyes in the intense cold. The face-mask protects your air-passages from infected dust, at the same time warming your inhaled breath and making you less liable to catch cold. Personally, I think these masks are one of the few really good things the Chinese Communist Party has introduced.

2

Formal and Political Education

I am not quite sure of all the subjects studied at the primary and middle-level schools in China, but I don't think they differ very much, with one exception, from those of most other countries. That exception is political indoctrination.

After middle school, the children may enter high school or get absorbed into productive labour in the factories and farms. High school studies are taken for three years to about the same level as that required for the Advanced level of the British General Certificate of Education, that is, to the level of the basic requirements for university entrance.

Chinese students are rather good at memory work. They have to be, for the very nature of their written language demands it. The Chinese language has no alphabet so you cannot spell words letter by letter as you would, for example, in English or French or in any African language. Every single Chinese sound is represented by a separate character, and the same sound, if it has more than one meaning, will be represented by more than one character. Although there is a limited number of basic sounds, there is no limit to the number of meanings and ideas that the basic sound can represent. Translation into Roman letters, even with appropriate letters, rather tends to complicate and destroy the beauty of the language. A word like *shi* may be accented and pronounced in four basic sounds, and may be written in at least fifty-eight different ways, each with a different name. Another word, *yi*, takes the usual four basic sounds, but may be written in at least forty-six different ways with just as many meanings. Whereas the Chinese ideogram simultaneously gives the meaning and the pronunciation of each word, a transliteration, when isolated, and even with proper accentuation, can at best only give the pronunciation, but with no precise idea of its meaning. It is something like having the English words 'saw' (past tense of verb to see) and 'saw' (carpenter's tool) written in isolation, or having 'right' (correct), 'right' (as opposed to left), 'right' (what one is entitled to), 'wright' (wheel-maker) and 'write' (present tense of verb to write) spoken in isolation. But in the case of transliterated Chinese words, this difficulty may be much greater.

Before you can count yourself literate in China, you have to memorise and be able instantly to recognise at least 1,500 different characters. This will just about enable you to read and write the most elementary material. For fluent reading of ordinary newspapers, magazines and books, you need to master at least 5,000 characters. I asked many times to know the total number of characters in the Chinese language, but nobody seemed to know even approximately. All I could learn was that the total runs to above 10,000. No wonder Chinese students are good at memory-work; you have to train yourself for it right from the start or else fall out.

In contrast to this, Chinese grammar is the simplest I have come across (I have a speaking and reading knowledge of Ewe, English, French, German and Chinese, and a reading knowledge of Spanish and Italian). It has no declensions or conjugations, and participles are not changed by the forms of nouns or verbs with which they are connected. Chinese is the sort of language you could master in a few months if it were not for the great obstacle presented by the large number of ideographic characters. If you can imagine a single character made up of about fifteen to twenty dots, dashes and curves, each of which has to occupy a definite position and run in a precise direction while maintaining a definite spatial relation to all the other dots, dashes and curves in the character, then you will be on the way to appreciating the difficulty that the written language presents.

The Chinese Communist Party has carried out at least one major reform in the language which has resulted in a considerable simplification and reduction in the number of the complicated characters of old. The régime is now planning to replace Chinese characters with the symbols of the Latin alphabet. But meanwhile the Chinese characters and the difficulty of mastering them remain.

*   *   *

Political education starts with formal education: at the earliest possible age. It begins with toddlers of between two and three years of age. In the kindergartens they are taught to sing revolutionary songs, to accept Mao Tse-tung as their father and to sing his praises, and to regard the American imperialists as the worst enemies of the Chinese people. I had a really big surprise the day I heard a little girl shout the slogan: '*dǎ dǎo měi dì guó zhǔ yì!*' (Down with American imperialism!); and this, mind you, from a little child who had hardly learned to speak coherently.

Why this preaching of hatred on such a large scale? The reasons, I think, are not far to seek. It's not only a question of the ideological conviction that America and other Western countries are enemies of communism.

The fact is, the New China has so many headaches and the people have so much to complain about that the Party must have something in addition to repression to keep them quiet. If the people can be made to believe that there is an external enemy always crying for their blood, it is then possible to impress on them that their survival as a people depends on government and people alike standing firmly together, no matter what happens. Hatred for the common enemy, for 'the imperialists headed by American imperialism', has helped to cement the people together in a way that brute force alone could not do. At times when an irremediable internal situation creates widespread discontent among the people and threatens the government's hold over them, all it needs to do is to step up the hatred campaign, invent new bogeys, and generally make the danger seem real enough to shake the people into forgetting their own grievances by rallying against the common enemy.

Of course, there is a reason other than political tactics or ideological fanaticism for the hate-campaign. Some Chinese (but not the Party) say that Taiwan (Formosa) has highly fertile land which would be theirs if China possessed the island. And it is the Americans who, by supporting Chiang Kai-shek, make Chinese conquest difficult and deprive the Chinese people of the good things the island could give them. So down with the Americans! This is hungry men's logic. But from the Party's viewpoint, I think, the Chinese plan to conquer Taiwan stems not so much from a desire to get control of a food-store once possessed long years ago by China as from a desire to communise Taiwan as part of a world-wide communist expansion. Laos, Thailand, South Vietnam and Cambodia are not 'integral parts' of China or the Soviet Union, but all nevertheless are subject to the pressure of communist expansion. Since the United

States and other Western countries stand in the way of this expansion, the Chinese have very real reason for hating the Western nations. Added to this is the régime's other motive—to use this hatred as a tactical diversion from internal difficulties.

This same technique of tactical diversion is beginning to be employed in African politics. Its success in China depends on two things: complete control of the press, and the political indoctrination of the people at all levels of their life, and especially at the level of school-life. How far are African imitators of the Chinese technique intending to go? There is immense enthusiasm in Africa for education, and any government which promises to pursue a far-reaching educational policy is sure to get massive support from the people. But what I want to know is: will it be education for a free Africa, or education for an Africa in which the people will become like the Chinese—docile and powerless pawns in the hands of their political bosses?

The Chinese régime is, of course, aware that large numbers of people would slip away from its doctrine if political education were to come to an end with the end of formal education. There is therefore no let-up at any time from political indoctrination. It goes on in one form or another until the individual is ready for his six feet of earth.

Both press and radio are monopolies of the Party in China. All news is rigorously censored. Any news about, for example, a rebellion in Tibet (the Tibetans are in a constant state of rebellion against a régime they never asked for and a system they do not want) is either entirely suppressed or toned down to give the impression that it is unrest by a handful of trouble-making reactionaries who have to be brought promptly to heel. News favourable to China, say a speech in praise of the country by a notable foreigner, is publicised, commented and recommented on for days on end. But the propaganda-din is loudest of all when there is some setback or internal trouble in a country in the anti-communist camp. A big strike in Japan or Britain or the United States pulls out all the stops on the radio and the press which hail it as heralding the victory of communism over capitalism. In expressing Chinese support for, and solidarity with, the strikers, the controllers of press and radio, of course, never lead the Chinese people into the error of thinking that there is any right to strike in the New China.

Newspapers and books from the outside world are not allowed in China unless they are published in socialist countries or are *bona fide* socialist papers published in capitalist countries (newspapers like *Humanité*, for example, the organ of the French Communist Party).

This policy is all part and parcel with the system of continual political education. To the Party, the people never leave school. In a sense, of course, people continue their political and civic education in democratic societies; there are always new things to be studied, new lessons to be learned, new problems to be understood. But where-as, in free societies, it is thought that people should be treated as adults in politics, in China it is thought they should be treated as rather stupid children and told by an ever-present schoolmaster what to think and what not to think. Even regarding democratic societies with a sceptical eye, one can say that, at least, there is more than one 'schoolmaster' laying down the law as to what the citizen should think. And the citizen can choose whether to listen to this 'schoolmaster' or not, or to none of them and set up his own 'school' of politics.

The perpetual censoring of what is learned in school and what is given in press and on the radio gives rise to a woeful ignorance of the world in which the Chinese

live. Time and time again, in arguing a particular point
in world politics, quite intelligent Chinese will say
things that one can only call, in the mildest terms, stupid.
They are never allowed to know what things are truly
like beyond their own frontiers. Even when they try
seriously to think about a particular problem in world
affairs, they have no grasp of the real facts because all facts
not favourable to communism are distorted at the start.
What is worse even than basing thinking on distorted
facts is the Party's deliberate discouragement of any independent thinking by the individual himself, either in the
classroom as a student or in home, social group or job as a
citizen. His business, as student and citizen, is to follow
the Party and obey it unquestioningly. This is hardly
calculated to train a man in logical reasoning or creative
thinking. It is calculated to make him an automaton
operated by the Party.

Just in case you have never been warned, I warn you
now never to argue politics with a Chinese communist,
particularly when the topic is Marxism. The unbrainiest
student in China has his belly so full of political texts
and copybook answers that he can knock a Churchill
through the ropes in debate. You may be even cleverer
than a Churchill, but I can promise you, when the bell
closes the contest, all you can say you have done is that
you came into contact with your opponent; you will have
made absolutely no impression on him, no matter how
well, how sincerely, how soundly you argued. Why?
Because you have been arguing with a closed mind, a
mind that believes that two and two make every conceivable sum except four if the Party line says so. From
his earliest infancy up, through all the grades of school
and then in adult life, he has it dinned into him that
communism is right, right and right again, right in big
things, right in small things, right in everything; and

B

everybody else is utterly and hopelessly and wickedly wrong.

During my early days in China, I spent hour after hour arguing with Chinese about the liberation of colonialist Africa. We would have probably made better progress in mutual understanding if I had been speaking Sanskrit (which I don't know) and they Hebrew (which they would hate to know). We just couldn't understand each other because, though our conversation at that time was entirely in English, we might just as well have been speaking different languages. By 'liberation', I meant getting rid of the colonialist masters. The same word 'liberation' for the Chinese meant turning a country communist. So, by their vocabulary, African countries like Nigeria, Sierra Leone, Congo and so on are still 'unliberated' and waiting for the glorious day of 'liberation', most likely by arms and technical assistance from China.

When it at last became clear to me what 'liberation' meant to them, it horrified me to think what it means for Africa. The apostles of Marx and Mao may well find it almost effortlessly easy to incite their disciples, crying the magic word 'liberation' to people for whom it means freedom from *all* oppression, to start a 'liberation crusade': the classical communist guerrilla war in Africa! God knows there is a lot we've got to do to make Africa free. But what sort of freedom can Africans expect from the hands of those who keep their own people in such subjection?

*   *   *

After kindergarten, children enter the primary and later the secondary schools, but politics never leave them at any stage. To the political songs and recitations of the nursery-school there are now added formal political lessons. There are lectures about the 'Three Red Banners' (the Great Leap Forward, the General Line, and the People's Communes) under which the People's Republic of China is carrying out her triumphant march towards socialism. Heavy stress is placed on the need for utter obedience to Mao Tse-tung and the Chinese Communist Party. When lessons are over, political education continues in the form of Youth Pioneer activities and lectures. Older Pioneers in the high school are promoted to membership of the Communist Youth League.

The most important criterion for admission into universities and higher institutions of education is not academic merit, but the level of 'socialist consciousness'. A candidate who in early days has been a Youth Pioneer and has become a Youth Leaguer in high school stands a very bright chance of admission into the university, whatever his intellectual ability. His training as a Pioneer and a Leaguer will have raised his socialist consciousness to such a degree that he will be ready to give unquestioning obedience to the Party. He will have been trained from an early age to relinquish to the Party the right to think any original thought. He is the man the Party wants, the man to whom higher education may be given with complete safety to the Party.

Another candidate who has hitherto not shown himself keenly participant in the Party's organisations or sufficiently responsive to its doctrines stands a very slim chance of gaining admission to a college or university. He will be regarded as a self-willed, independent thinker, the type whom the Party has every reason to suspect. Higher education for him could be dangerous for the Party.

From the academic viewpoint, such a system of selection is very unsatisfactory, to put it mildly, since it is

usually the mediocre and lazy brains who make good
party-faithfuls, while better minds prefer intellectual
independence. This system therefore pushes into institutions of higher education large numbers of students
with mediocre brains, people who are content to
remain in the rut of routine rather than to experiment
and initiate creative ideas.

Seeing the results of this system in China has increased my disquiet over signs of its developing in
Africa. When the government of Ghana, for example,
enacted a law requiring that all foreign scholarships be
channelled through the government for award to suitable
candidates, it was generally thought that 'suitable'
meant 'academically suitable'. But there is evidence to
suggest that it is being taken to mean 'capable of further-
ing the ruling party's cause'. I would like to think my
own experience of this sort of thing was exceptional, but
I've now regretfully come to the conclusion that it is be-
coming the rule. When I applied for the scholarship
which finally took me to China, the first question asked
of me was whether I'd got a membership card of the
government party. It was suggested I had better 'arrange'
to get one. So I did. It wasn't difficult to find a party
secretary, for the fee of one bottle of gin, to issue me a
party-card, back-dating it two years on receipt of the
registration dues for that period. I was burningly keen to
get the scholarship and so signed on the dotted line. A
silly formality, involving just a little mild corruption?
Perhaps; but, looking back, it seems to me that, in
principle, the only thing differentiating what was required of me from what is required of Chinese students
is the bottle of gin. They have to give cast-iron proof of
their loyalty to the Party in order to get the benefits of
higher education, scholarships and so forth. How long
will it take for African imitators of the system to operate

it in grim earnest and demand stronger proof of loyalty to the régime in power than a bottle of gin placed in the right hands at the right time?

*   *   *

It is at college and university level that Chinese students are formally introduced to Marx, Engels, Lenin and Mao Tse-tung. Every student, no matter what course he is taking, has to attend four to five hours of compulsory political lectures each week. A student is expected to take his political lectures, if anything, more seriously than his course lectures. Students who get consistently low marks in political studies run the risk, no matter how good they are at their speciality, of expulsion to the collective farms. On the other hand, students who shine in the political course, however dim and backward in their formal studies, can be assured of high favour with their superiors.

I have to explain that the term 'politics', in this context, is used in quite a different sense from its normal meaning in the Western academic world. In a Western-style university, a student of politics studies the different political systems, comparing and contrasting them; he seeks to make out the advantages and disadvantages of each, to evaluate them in the light of their theory and practice and in their various historical and social contexts. He is taught the discipline of critical enquiry and to examine the various political systems impartially and without respect to the feelings or bias of any one professor or student.

But in Chinese education, 'politics' means Marxism as expounded, commented on and interpreted by Marx, Engels, Lenin and Mao Tse-tung. Other political systems are considered only in the light of Marxism and are judged solely by Marxist criteria. Anything written by these revered leaders of Marxist thought is all-good and unquestionably correct; anything from a different school of thought is all-bad or, at best, grossly imperfect. Such meagre attention as is given to non-Marxist political theories is so fragmentary and biased that political studies in China can give even the most intelligent student only a woefully lopsided view of the world.

School textbooks, and every other kind of book for that matter, all go through the censor's mill. All the textbooks now used in schools have been rewritten to give them a Marxist bias because there may be in the old books ideas that conflict with party doctrine. It is the same with fiction; everything an author writes must reflect the Party's attitude. If a writer is so foolhardy as to express opinions which run counter to what the Party says in any matter, two results will follow for certain: the book will never be published, of course; and the author will end up doing several years in labour and 'political re-education' camps. If he is lucky enough to get out of these alive, and still wants to continue as a writer, then what you will get from him will be books praising the Chinese Communist Party to high heaven.

The thing goes so far that any new book you open seems to have the same theme as the one you have just closed. This is why I find it hard to work up much interest in novels published in mainland China. They are dull and uninteresting, with nothing original or fresh in them; just the old, old story.

There was a time when I went in for buying large numbers of little illustrated books: the sort of thing which, here in Africa or other parts of the world, would be called comic books, only in China they cannot be called such because they contain no humour at all. They are simply bursting with politics, hidden or overt. One of these little books was telling me of a former soldier in the Liberation Army who, after demobilisation, became a rag-picker for one of the state textile factories. This man, the little book said, was so expert in domestic economy that he made his shirt (he had only one) last him ten solid years. The little book did not specify what material that shirt was made of, but I'll bet it must have been made of chain-mail, the sort of shirt that would have delighted Don Quixote.

The fact is, of course, that clothing materials had become scarce and the people could not get any more than two feet of cloth per person per annum. So the Party adopted this method of conveying to them the sad fact that they had better make their shirts last longer, for they were not likely to get another one in the foreseeable future.

I remember the day my class in the Institute of Foreign Languages was issued with copies of a new textbook for chemistry. We were near the completion of our language course and were being given some coaching in technical vocabulary. The first chapter of the book gave the definition of matter. It began: 'Lenin said . . .' and there then followed something that Comrade Lenin considered to be the correct definition of matter. But this definition conflicted so violently with everything I had learned before that I promptly raised the point with the instructor. She explained to me, very patiently, that what our class was expected to do was to master some technical terms; we were not to worry about Lenin's definition of matter. And so I stopped worrying. But millions of high-school students all over China have really got something to worry about; that book is their foundation textbook in chemistry. Now, of course, whatever you may think of his doctrines, you will be right in thinking that Lenin is a very important political thinker. But did you know he was also a great physicist and chemist? You didn't? Well, the Chinese Communist Party says he is, and the Party must be right, whatever the rest of the world says!

Chinese universities and colleges very rightly pay great attention to the natural sciences, to medicine, agricultural science and to technology. These are important branches of learning in their own right and are particularly important to China in her efforts at socialist reconstruction. They concentrate on these studies. Any subject not directly connected with industrialisation or food production is considered 'useless'. So if you are aiming at going to China to study economics, anthropology, sociology or any of the liberal arts, you had better think again for either these things are not catered for in Chinese education or they are narrowly treated from a doctrinaire Marxist viewpoint. The study of history is limited to the history of communism, more specifically that of the Chinese Communist Party, while studies in politics won't take you further than Marx, Engels, Lenin and Mao Tse-tung.

Close to the Peking Medical College in the northern outskirts of the city I once saw a notice-board announcing in bright red letters that behind the walls was a school of law. Exactly what they study in that place I never discovered. But this much I am certain of: it couldn't be anything connected with the art of advocacy or any allied subject. The process of administering justice in Chinese courts consists of asking the accused to confess to the charge made against him. Should the accused delay his confession, there are many refined ways, in which the Chinese are expert, of 'persuading' him to hasten matters. What has a trained lawyer to do in such a court?

In just the same way as books are controlled, professors

and all whose business it is to teach are subject to control in what they teach. I came across a striking example of this in the Peking Medical College. Our biology professor was lecturing to us on metabolism. There was every indication that she was an expert in her subject (she had studied, I believe, in the United States before China's 'liberation'). Yet she told us that, because proteins, fats and carbohydrates are inter-convertible during human metabolic processes, the people of China therefore do not suffer any nutritional loss in consequence of their diet's deficiency in fats and proteins. This is as much as to say that all the advice doctors and experts in nutrition give us about the importance of mixed diets to our health is just flat nonsense. I did not blame her then, nor do I blame her now. She was not telling us what she knew to be a fact, but rather what she had been ordered to tell us as a political necessity. It's not surprising she could not look us in the face as she was telling us this tripe nor make what she said sound convincing.

All this is easily understood by those who know something of the situation in China. Faced with a super-acute shortage of protein foods (meat, eggs, milk) and fats, the Party declares that these things are no longer really necessities, but are luxuries which the Chinese people can well do without. The people accordingly must be persuaded to accept an all-carbohydrate and nutritionally useless roughage diet until an improvement in the food situation occurs which will then permit the Party to change its line and 'demote' meat, eggs and milk from the remote pinnacle of luxury to the lowlier position of necessity. The fat-protein 'grapes' became sour!

And, mark you, this lecture on metabolism was one of the foundation-stones on which I was expected to build my medical studies. Chinese doctors are safe from

ridicule in their own country because everyone is taught
to accept the same standard lie. But I should be hooted at
with contempt if I voiced such an idea outside China.
This distortion of what I knew to be scientific fact
cropped up within my first days at the Medical School.
I began to wonder how many more lay ahead and what
use my studies there were going to be to me in the
profession I wanted to follow.

There were numerous incidents that did much to shake
my confidence in the teachers and the College. I can't
cite them all here, for they are too many; I shall mention
just one more.

It happened when I went for the first time to the
organic chemistry laboratory. That afternoon we were
conducting an experiment to determine the melting
point of some organic chemical. The first thing, before
fixing the apparatus, was to check the accuracy of the
thermometer we were to use. As every student of
elementary chemistry knows (or should know), this is
done by holding the bulb of the thermometer in escaping
steam in a vessel. If, when the water is boiling, the
thermometer-reading stands and remains at 100°C, the
graduation is accurate.

We students were working in pairs, each pair to a set
of apparatus. But before we started the experiment, I had
an argument with my partner about how the apparatus
should be fixed for checking the accuracy of the thermometer. He stoutly maintained that, since we were
taking the temperature of water, the bulb of the thermometer should be immersed in the boiling water. That,
of course, would have been correct enough if only
approximate results, not strict scientific accuracy, were
required. But we were supposed to be checking the
scientific accuracy of our thermometer, and any factor
which could give rise to an erroneous reading had to be

carefully eliminated. The water we were using was ordinary tap-water containing dissolved chemical impurities; our flask still had irremovable deposits in it from previous experiments; and, moreover, water is liable to superheating (i.e. heating above 100°C without boiling) under some conditions. So I argued that the best method was to keep the thermometer bulb well above the water, in the stream of escaping steam. He didn't look convinced, neither did the other students who had stopped their experiments to listen to us. But in the end he reluctantly allowed me to arrange the apparatus my own way. I did. But shortly after, the supervising laboratory technician came round, took one look at our set-up and told me the arrangement of my apparatus was dead wrong. I tried to explain, but it was no good. She took the same line as my partner: the bulb must be immersed in the water. I was the only foreign student among all the Chinese in that laboratory group, and my Chinese was rather inadequate for scientific argument; I gave up.

But as soon as the class ended, I dashed to my room and took down two of my chemistry textbooks printed in English, borrowing two more from a Nepalese friend, and feverishly examined them. All four books showed I was right. I took them off straightaway to the dormitory of my Chinese partner in the experiment and showed him the authorities for my case. Would he do the same for his? He couldn't.

A fortnight later, another organic chemistry experimentation class came round. The technical instructor who had made the mistake was no longer there. I never saw her again till I left the college. There was another experiment on melting point that day. Her replacement took care to explain to us the right way to fix the thermometer and why. Everything she said was a repetition of the arguments I had previously put forward. I didn't expect either apology or explanation, and none was offered.

By itself, this incident may not be of much consequence, and I do not cite it to boast a petty triumph. I refer to it because it was one of the links in the chain of events which eventually sent me packing home. Professors and technical instructors were people whose authority I had been taught to respect. Yet early on in my studies, I had been required to swallow three statements with no basis in scientific fact. In the case of Lenin's definition of matter, the lecture on metabolism and the affair of the thermometer, quite elementary questions were involved which I could quite easily check up on for myself. But the thought knocked at my mind: if in such elementary things I had come across mistakes and deception, what was I to expect when it came to higher things about which I had no previous knowledge or easy means of checking? Would the medicine taught me by the Chinese be acceptable back home where I was to practise after my studies?

Added to this growing concern over the quality of the instruction at the Peking Medical School was a certain uneasiness over the fact that Chinese universities do not grant degrees, only diplomas. This is the case in all branches of study. A degree, of course, is at best only a rough guide to what the degree-holder can be assumed to know. Many a man with a string of high-sounding abbreviations after his name sags like an empty sack when put to the test.

All the same, in most universities of the world the existence of degrees implies a high level of intellectual discipline and assessment of students' capacities. The absence of degrees in China was one of the main grievances of the first batch of twelve African students who left China for home towards the end of 1960. I found this question bulked large in the complaints of the only Rhodesian student who arrived towards the close of 1961 to study medicine. The look of the Medical College did not inspire much confidence in him, and when he learnt that he would not be awarded a degree at the end of his studies, he decided he was wasting his time in China, for, without a degree, there was little chance of his obtaining recognition at home as a qualified doctor. I can confirm that this is the case in most African countries. I was in Lagos, Nigeria, when an Indian (or Pakistani; I forget which) declared he was going to start a protest fast outside the Prime Minister's residence. He had been offered a job in a private school only to find on arrival in Nigeria that he wouldn't be able to take it up since his degree was not recognised. We may be rightly sceptical about paper qualifications, but how far can we afford to disregard the usages of the community in which we hope to live and work?

It is not easy for me to say whether the abolition of academic degrees in China is just a measure aimed at doing away with fancy academic titles and thus promoting the greater aim of social equality. I rather doubt that this is the case since the official explanation is that the non-award of degrees 'is in consonance with the socialist educational policy of China'. This would seem to indicate that the purpose of the change is primarily educational rather than social.

I got an unofficial explanation from a student friend in Peking. According to him, communist students in the early days of the régime were so busy watching over the socialist consciousness of their non-communist fellows that they had little time left for attending to formal academic studies. The result was that the non-communist students, who asked only to be left alone with their studies, began to beat their communist comrades in examinations to such an extent as to alarm the Party. To prevent 'loss of face', diplomas were substituted for degrees. In awarding these diplomas, the level of socialist consciousness in a given student is considered even more important than his scholastic achievement; so it is impossible for party-members to lose face.

I am inclined to accept this non-official explanation because it rings true with my own experience of education in China. What worried me and other foreign students was the debasement of academic standards consequent on the abolition of degrees. How far would a Chinese diploma in medicine be acceptable back at home? Of course, if the medicine the Chinese could teach me were superior or at least comparable to that taught in the West, then there would probably not be much difficulty in getting myself recognised as a competent doctor on my own merits. But if, as it seemed after my first weeks in the college, it was questionable whether my training would match, much less surpass, that of doctors trained in other countries, what then would be my fate on returning home? After six years of gruelling study, what if I were to arrive back in Ghana only to find that the government which gave a verbal promise to take me into its service on the strength of a diploma only, had changed its policy in favour of medical graduates with degrees recognised as of high standing by the world of medicine? As I pursued my studies in Peking, these anxieties were increased. They were not allayed by my ordinary day-to-day experiences as a student.

*   *   *

Life on a Chinese campus has some rather striking characteristics, the main one being that students are expected to live like Spartans. In the Institute of Foreign Languages, overseas students lived separately from the Chinese, so foreigners did not really have a proper opportunity to learn about the life of Chinese students. It was only when I entered the medical college that I got to know about university life in China. What I saw came as a pretty sharp shock.

Groups of eight students occupy a room of ten feet by twelve feet, sleeping in tiered bunks. Their personal belongings—boxes, bags, books and clothing—are stacked higgledy-piggledy in any available corner. For lack of space, there are no tables, no chairs, no bookshelves. When they need to sit, they crouch down on the lower bunks and do their private study in the lecture halls. The room has one door and one window. In winter, the window is kept shut and sealed with wedges of newspaper; the door is always kept closed because of the cold. With eight people, those rooms get very stuffy! Each accommodation block has three floors; each floor, containing nearly 150 students, has one washroom and a lavatory with five cubicles. In some of the cubicles, the water system is permanently out of order. The result is rather hideous. Throughout my stay in the college I never once smelt any kind of disinfectant anywhere, though the need for it was urgent. On the floor where I lived (in Block 5–2, which was mainly occupied by foreign students: Nepalese, Indonesians, Albanians, Vietnamese and myself, the lone African in college) every student swept his own room and left the rubbish in the corridor. The comrade charwoman cleaned the corridors during teaching hours in the morning. On Sunday she had her day-off and the corridor got bestrewn with rubbish. I forbear to repeat the caustic comments of Sunday visitors, many of them diplomatists; the best that can be said is that the living quarters of the

Chinese students were a good deal more squalid.

The lecture halls were swept once a week, on Saturday afternoons. It is not easy to describe the squalor of those halls by Friday afternoon and Saturday morning. It was enough to appal a foreign layman, let alone a foreign doctor. You haven't forgotten, of course, that this place is a medical college, the place where China's doctors and medical personnel are trained. In winter, many of the students catch cold. Phlegm and sputum are spat on the floor indiscriminately during lectures. Offenders are never rebuked. Everybody seems to regard spitting as normal; except we foreigners, of course.

The teaching staff are a little better accommodated. Three or four bachelor professors and lecturers share a room. They sleep on camp-beds and their room may have one or two small tables with matching chairs. There is not much else by way of amenities and certainly nothing which could be regarded as approaching comfort.

There are about 5,000 students in the college (though the number may have increased since I was there), and all eat in one dining hall which also does duty as assembly hall, theatre, indoor gamesroom and so forth. Lecturers who are not party-members also eat in this hall.

The relationship between students and tutors is the closest thing to social equality I saw in socialist China. But the officials running educational institutions, party-members with hardly any exception, stand outside this relationship.

The whole college has only one bath-house, which serves professors, technical assistants and students alike. The bath-house is divided into two compartments: a small section with six bath-tubs for members of the staff, and a larger compartment containing twenty-six showers for the 5,000 students. If you are inclined to say, 'come off it', let me tell you I found it so strange that I went round and counted them. Of these twenty-six showers, one was permanently out of order during the whole of my stay in the college. The same bath-house serves men and women alike, so an arrangement is worked out to avoid embarrassing clashes. On one day, men bath between midday and two o'clock; women between five and seven-thirty in the evening. The following day the order is reversed: women in the afternoon, men in the evening. The college has about as many women as men. The mind boggles at the thought of what would happen if all of the 2,500 men decided to have their bath on the same day and within two hours. Each person would have seventy-two seconds to undress, bath, dry, dress and get out. In winter, one can get by with a bath a week perhaps, but in the hot sweltering summer . . . ! Many foreign students found the hygiene in this bath-house so unimpressive that they refused to bath there, preferring to go quite long distances to their respective embassies to cadge a bath.

Do you think I'm being unduly critical? Well, of course, it would be foolish to expect elaborate amenities in the universities of a country which is struggling to raise itself from the dust of backwardness. A life of austerity is concomitant with that struggle. And in China, which for centuries has known huge mass populations and is now experiencing a fantastic 'population explosion', over-crowding has to be accepted as a norm of life. Through long experience, the Chinese can adapt themselves to conditions which would daunt people of other countries. But while poverty is no crime and austere living conditions no disgrace, there is no excuse for dirt and squalor. The conditions I met with are such as could easily have been remedied by a government more concerned with the welfare of its people and less with

expenditure on aid to communist guerrillas in other
countries and on military preparations for domineering
over and annexing weaker neighbours.

A Chinese girl student once said, quite bluntly, that
Africa is universally known as the most backward continent on earth. I come from this 'primitive backwater',
and I can say that, so far as accommodation for higher as
well as lower institutions of learning is concerned, and
in what relates to personal and general hygiene and the
treatment of students as human beings, it is we Africans
who must civilise the Chinese, not *vice versa*.

*   *   *

In the dormitories, students are under the supervision of
members of the Communist Youth League whose duty
it is to watch over the level of socialist consciousness of
their fellow students. Each class is nominally headed by a
prefect but is really controlled by a political representative
who is either a full member of the Communist Party, or
a member of the Youth League.

The Chinese delight in saying that such and such a
good thing was done 'under the leadership of the Party'.
It is for the same reason that train crews, hospital staff
and the personnel of every conceivable institution have
to be under the control of party-representatives. I
remember reading in one of my language textbooks of a
steel worker in Shanghai who was severely burnt in an
accident at work. As they rushed him to hospital, he
kept calling out in his coma: 'I want to live, I want to
live. Steel needs me, steel needs me.' This sounded a bit
improbable to me, but that was what the textbook said.
While the patient waited, the Party's agent attached
to the hospital thought it necessary first to call a meeting
of all the doctors and staff. He gave them a long harangue

which in substance amounted to this: under the leadership of the Party, this man has to be saved at all costs.
The doctors were finally released from the meeting and
went into action. After a series of operations, skin-grafts
and blood transfusions and many months of anxiety,
the man's life was saved. In the opinion of some foreign
doctors, the Chinese did a really brilliant job. The lesson
we were to draw from this story was that in socialist
countries doctors give disinterested service to their
patients, whereas in capitalist countries they are only
interested in money, and that without the Party's
leadership the man's life would never have been saved.
But I somehow doubt if a man's life can be saved, however
inspiring the 'leadership of the Party', if the doctor
in the first place does not have the know-how. And I
certainly question the wisdom of leaving a patient to
await treatment to enable his doctors to listen to a long
harangue from an official of the Party.

Chinese campuses do not have debating societies, music
and dancing clubs and all the multitude of different
clubs and societies that enliven university life and make it
something to remember long after college days are
over. There is only one society: the Communist Youth
League. During my first weeks in the Language Institute, life was so unbearably dull that I asked the dean of
the Foreign Students' Department to introduce us to
some clubs we could join. He replied that we must wait
until we knew enough Chinese. But when I had learned
the language, I didn't trouble the dean with this question
a second time; I had by then discovered that there were
no student societies other than the Youth League.

The two favourite sports in China are table-tennis and
basket-ball, but in many cases the basket-ball pitches
have been taken over for cultivation. Hunger has

driven the students to convert almost all their playing
fields into vegetable gardens. Football is also played, but
usually by foreign students—African, European and
Korean. Badminton and volley-ball complete, I think,
the list of games available. Field athletics come very
low down in the list. At no time during my stay in the
country did I see or hear of inter-college sports com-
petitions of any sort, and certainly I detected none of that
friendly inter-campus rivalry which puts so much healthy
pep into college life. The students were obviously too
busy growing cabbages to think of such frivolities.

With only one exception, I saw or heard nothing of
any arrangements for extra-mural studies. There are no
courses arranged during the summer vacation, which
lasts forty-five days. I did once read in an illustrated
magazine about an extra-mural physics course con-
ducted by television. But in a country where television
sets are as rare as dogs and cats (which have been killed
off and eaten for lack of beef and pork), this struck me as
just so much propaganda for foreign consumption.

Paradoxically, for all the emphasis on collective acting
and thinking, I never got the impression of belonging to
a corporate life. Even without sports activities or degree-
giving assemblies, one would have thought there would
have been occasions when the university forgathered as
a body to do something interesting, academically or
socially. But the Chinese don't waste their time on
convocation ceremonies. What comes closest to it is the
assembly of a whole teaching institution on New Year's
Eve. I was present at the one held in the Language
Institute at New Year, 1961. The president mounted the
platform in the hall that does service also as dining and
lecture hall, and amidst loud applause began his speech.
It was what you would have expected from any run-of-
the-mill party-secretary. He churned out all the stock

statements of the Party. He told us that the East wind was prevailing over the West wind, and how happy the Chinese people were under the leadership of the Party and all about the Great Leap Forward. We'd all heard this sort of thing time and time again. In a speech from the head of your college, you look for something relevant to your life as a student, something to set your brain working. But not if you are at a Chinese university or college. This president of ours, like his colleagues in other teaching institutions, was just a stalwart of the Party who had been rewarded with a job. Had he been an academic, as he should have been, had he been free to speak his mind, he would have told us something original instead of merely reproducing stereotyped party propaganda. Even if he had thought a strictly academic theme inappropriate for the occasion, there was, heaven knows, plenty of material to hand for an interesting discourse on the current situation in China: the problems encountered in promoting the people's communes, the setback to the Great Leap Forward and the measures necessary for avoiding such setbacks in the future, and so on. However devoted to the régime, an intellectually capable president could have at least given an interesting address to this one annual assembly of the whole institute. But no; he just stood there shouting: 'Long live the people's communes!' The Party at that time had not officially condemned the commune idea, and I suppose that if our president had dared to wish anything other than long life to the people's communes, he would have been reduced to the status of a peasant in one of them. He had to toe the party-line in order to retain his post as a fifteen-kilograms-of-meat-a-month president of a college.

*　　　*　　　*

A man may seek education because it puts in his hand a tool for supporting himself and his dependants in life. He may also seek it because it prepares him to give of his best to his country. A man may also want education because it enables him to lead a richer, fuller and more meaningful life. These aims may be mixed in varying proportions in different individuals.

Chinese education today is solely concerned with preparing the individual for service to his country. His personal predilections and feelings do not enter into consideration. Yet even in this undesirably narrow aim, Chinese education fails miserably because of its excessive emphasis on politics and on intellectual enslavement.

Country first! A noble aim; but this should be a matter of voluntary choice, not of compulsion. No man ever works so well as when he works with a will. Even asses refuse to work when they don't want to, and camels will not budge when mercilessly overloaded. I have a deep pity for those whose educational system denies them the right to choose, whose 'choice' of study, of profession, amounts to some superior body's choice which they are forced to accept. It is a woeful thing for humanity when men in power anywhere in the world begin to rate their fellow men below asses and camels.

3

Social Structure

Socialist China is a classless society. You have heard that
before, no doubt. If ever there was a barefaced lie, this is
it. From my own observation, I distinguished four main
strata.

At the very top of China's new social structure stand
the highest communist bosses, the immediate associates
and henchmen of Mao Tse-tung and members of the
highest organs of Party and State. They are very
privileged people. In the midst of China's present dire
want of food, clothing and other consumer commodities,
the members of this boss class can obtain anything they
want which is at all obtainable in the country. There are
special shops which cater for their private needs; shops
which are barred to the general public. You have perhaps heard some people praise the excellence of Chinese
dishes. These special dishes are what the bosses and their
families eat at home, and it is to these that foreign
guests are treated at official and private banquets.
There are available for them special cigarettes, the best
and costliest in the land. The ordinary Chinese cannot
obtain them, even if they had the money. As I have
already mentioned, the high-ups, though wearing the
same eternal blue of all the Chinese, dress in clothes of a
cut and quality unobtainable by the rest of the people.

These people form New China's 'aristocracy'. Going
along the street, you often see a Soviet-style car with

curtains drawn. Behind these curtains sits one of the aristocrats of this 'classless society', screened off from the teeming masses whose business it is to submit to being bossed.

Below this 'aristocracy', there is the secondary stratum, a sort of 'gentry' made up of people, mostly members of the Party, who hold prominent posts as presidents of universities, heads of large factories and other state organisations. They also have many privileges which distinguish them from the masses: cars and allowances for more and better food, the right to shop at special stores and so forth.

Beneath them there is the new 'middle class' consisting of the rank and file of the Communist Party, at the head of which is a sort of 'upper' middle class consisting of party-secretaries and leading cadres and the managers and supervisors of communes and small factories. They have no clearly defined special privileges that I know of, but the password 'I am a party-member' is an open sesame to many doors, and the more resourceful members of this class are able to gain many advantages for themselves on the side. Moreover, since membership of the Party is granted solely as a reward for special merit or outstanding services to the communist cause, even an ordinary member of the Party considers himself to be elevated high above the masses by mere virtue of this party-membership, just as many an Englishman considers himself a cut above his fellows if he can add an OBE or KCMG after his name. Whatever the rights and wrongs of awarding special distinctions to people, the fact that party-membership carries with it a special social status makes the régime's claim that China is a classless society a pretty cynical exercise in humbug. The relationship between party-member and commoner becomes that of superior and inferior.

Crushed at the botton of this social pyramid are the masses (and incidentally, by 'masses', the Chinese communist means everybody not belonging to the Party). The workers and peasants feel everyone's foot but can kick back at no one. Whenever there is a shortage of anything, it is they who must bear the brunt. They eat the worst and least nourishing foods, mostly cabbage—cabbage for lunch, cabbage for supper; cabbage yesterday, cabbage today and cabbage tomorrow. They wear the poorest clothes, smoke the cheapest and most evil-smelling cigarettes and drink the vilest concoction imaginable which is misnamed wine. Underfed, ill-clothed, it is for them that the heaviest drudgery, the most back-breaking tasks, are reserved, in the name of that communist system which is supposed to have been adopted first and foremost for their special benefit.

Among the masses, there used to be a small but noticeable sub-division, the white-collar and factory workers. In the Party's view, they proved to be lacking in 'socialist consciousness' for they regarded themselves as a separate group, distinct from and superior to the peasantry. China's aristocracy is a very jealous class and will allow no superior or bossy airs to any save the Party. Such dangerous 'bourgeois' tendencies amongst industrial and clerical workers were put down a few years ago by a regulation ordaining that they must go back to the land for a stated period once a year. This measure also proved serviceable for keeping intellectuals in their place. On the whole, the most fanatical and, therefore, best, communists are the uneducated and the semi-educated. Men and women of a certain intellectual standing are not so completely reliable. Since it is common in China to find heads of colleges and factories who have no intellectual or managerial competence worth mentioning, because appointment to leading posts is based on political

qualifications first and foremost, a good many intellectuals
and technically competent people turn up their noses at
these oafs who lord it over them. Toiling with the
peasants is reckoned a good way to curb the high-
flying notions of intellectuals and specialists by showing
them where the power lies.

But this is probably thought of by the régime as an
incidental merit of the 'back to the land' policy. There
must have been a good deal of nose-raising by intellectuals
before this measure was introduced; its promulgation
coincided with the extremely acute food shortage. But
China's leaders, faced with this appalling problem of
their own making, are very reluctant to admit to the
outside world that food is so short that millions have to be
imported from the towns into the country to dig and hoe.
The whole operation is put over as an exercise in socialist
co-operation. Even Chairman Mao and his colleagues
often perform publicity stunts, going to work with
peasants. When this happens the propaganda din from
Radio Peking and the newspapers simply deafens you.
My Chinese textbook carries a story which relates that
when a bus-load of Chairman Mao and other leaders of
the party arrived at the site of the Dam of the Thirty
Tombs, one old man burst into a flood of tears and cried:
'At this very spot, the emperors forced our fathers to
build tombs. Today Chairman Mao, busy as he is, still
snatches some time to come and help us build a dam and
reap richer harvests. Oh, the Party's goodness is infinite!'
Chairman Mao held the spade for about one hour and
fifty minutes; the masses toil from dawn to dusk, for
months and years on end.

*   *   *

There is one other class in China, a non-indigenous class.
It consists of foreigners. These are very few in number,

but for political reasons the Party has raised them to a
special status which is approximately equal to that of the
rank and file of the Communist Party. Diplomatists,
visiting foreigners, resident technical experts from other
socialist countries and foreign students, especially those
from Africa and Europe, belong to this class. Foreign
diplomatists usually can get preference over the ordinary
Chinese in food and commodities which are available.
But because of the acute shortage of consumer commodities, they all prefer, including those from socialist
countries, to order the bulk of their commodities from
the British territory of Hong Kong.

China, before the communists took over, suffered from
a plague of foreigners who occupied special enclaves and
acquired special rights and concessions, including extra-
territorial rights. Their warships sailed up and down
Chinese waters with impunity. The Communist Party
zealously lead the masses in the 'resolute struggle'
against these imperialist oppressors. The Party triumphed.
The Chinese people ousted the *wài guó gǔi zě*—the
foreign devils—from these enclaves and positions of
privilege. All this and much more my language textbooks told me. The Chinese guides on my tour in south
China did not neglect to show me the park where once a
notice proclaimed: 'Chinese and dogs not admitted.'

But twelve years after the glorious liberation, this very
party which led the Chinese masses in the struggle against
the foreigners' special privileges turned yet another of its
political somersaults and lo! foreigners were back again
with special privileges. Only this time it was not a case of
the foreigners demanding privileges. The Party spoke
and privileges came to the foreigners.

Foreign students can get good food and good clothes;
they can also smoke good cigarettes of the same quality
as those of the aristocrats. If they fancy a drink, they

can buy the mellowest red wine and best Chinese vodka
in the land.

And why not? How else could the Party blind us to the
misery of the common people? How else could we
students be made to swallow the communist pill? And
why then should they consider China a hell compared to
other countries they know? I am writing this book to say
why.

*   *   *

One of the most potent arguments the communists
evoke in their attempt to convert the African to their
ideology is the argument against inequality: inequality
of wealth, of opportunity and so on. It is important
therefore to know how far they themselves succeed in
practising social equality.

China of old had her emperors, mandarins, officials and
landlords. All these classes of people, I learnt from the
history books, were very tyrannical and cruel to the
common people. They wallowed in wealth and plenty
while the common people, the toiling masses, could
hardly manage one square meal a day. A redistribution
of land and of wealth seemed clearly desirable to ensure
that the rich were not too rich nor the poor too poor. The
Chinese Communist Party promised to the peasants the
abolition of the class system and the introduction of social
equality for all. Certainly, the Party exterminated the
landlords (it went a good deal further than simply
abolishing the class of landlords) and despotic rulers.
That was the first step to fulfilling its promise to the
masses.

But what has happened since? Do the communist
leaders not occupy the very same palaces and villas from
which the mandarins and landlords were evicted and

murdered? Do they not now lead a life of plenty, as once did the landlords, while the masses hunger? Do they not now scorn the masses and trample on their rights? Where then lies the social equality?

Not only China, but all the other countries of the communist bloc have had the same experience. The establishment of a 'people's socialist state' breaks down the old social order, but never fails to set up a new superior class, and one which in many more ways than the old has proved to be ruthless and tyrannical.

African society certainly has many evils that our nation-builders, politicians and commoners alike must work hard to correct. But in my view it is wrong to think that communism in itself is such a potent panacea that its advent alone can rid our countries of all that we have most reason to deplore. While I have no doubt that there are some useful things we can learn from the communists (no system can ever be so bad as to be totally bad), I maintain that any talk of social equality which comes from the communists and is aimed at us Africans is about as good as the advice a tiger can give to a cow about vegetable diets—just so much rubbish.

4

The People's Communes

If there is anything in China that people in other countries most widely discuss and speculate on, it is the people's communes. But, if you have heard anything about them, the chances are that your facts are dead wrong. The fact is, the people's communes are washed out, but the Communist Party sees fit to keep silent about their demise. Foreign visitors are still fed stale and misleading propaganda about the success and glory of these communes, so I owe it to my readers to tell what I know of them.

The commune system is not completely a Chinese idea. It was tried in the Soviet Union on an experimental scale and found unworkable. Hence the Chinese boast that, in establishing the communes on a nation-wide scale, they have gone one step ahead of the Soviet Union in the march towards the communist ideal.

But the boast is a bit premature; it is one thing to introduce a new system, and quite another thing to make it work. The Soviet Union was supposed to be China's best friend; at least the two kept up friendly appearances fairly well. It was therefore no end of a surprise to me to discover in my travels in the USSR that one of the biggest jokes in the Soviet 'gag book' was the flop of the Chinese people's communes. Everyone who got to know that I had just left China brought up the topic of the communes, and the laughter was uproarious. Even stranger: Soviet citizens I met on the Trans-Siberian railway unhesitatingly chorused their agreement when I stated my conviction that Red China is a positive disgrace to socialism.

This is the same Red China, mark you, which holds herself up to us Africans as a paragon of socialist progress, as the example Africa must follow. There are some in prominent positions in Africa who are keen to copy China's example. All I can say is that on their visits they must only have listened to the official Chinese line. I had the advantage of listening to the point of view of the ordinary Chinese.

I should like to start my story where it really should begin—in the period immediately before the communist take-over.

The population of China throughout the ages has consisted of an overwhelming proportion of peasants. Before the victory of Mao's movement, the country had a minority landlord class which owned almost all the land. The landlords themselves did not cultivate their land; they rented it out to peasants. Many of the peasants were so hopelessly poor that they could not afford even the simplest tools used in primitive cultivation—hoes, spades and so forth. Land and tools all belonged to the landlords, whose merciless exploitation meant that many peasant families could scarcely manage one square meal a day. In winter they lacked warm clothes and fuel. In times of serious crop failure millions of them died of starvation. The peasants in this dire plight were classified by the Communist Party as 'poor peasants'.

A second class of peasants, the 'middle-level peasants', had tiny plots of their own which they cultivated with their own simple implements. Some of these middle-level peasants might own 'one leg of cattle' (the Chinese expression), meaning that four people own, say, one ox in common; each is said to own one leg.

There was a smaller third class, called by the Party 'rich peasants'. These had rather larger plots of land and usually a plough and some draught animals. In some cases they cultivated their land with the help of a few hired labourers.

The poor peasants and labourers so far outnumbered the middle-level and rich peasants that the whole country could correctly be described as one vast milling mass of empty bellies. Even to this day, one of the traditional forms of greeting in China is: 'Have you eaten?' to which the reply is 'not yet' or 'already'.

When the Communist Party came and promised the peasants a redistribution of land, ensuring that everyone had a fair share, this was to offer them paradise for living hell. They rallied solidly behind the Party in the areas where it exercised effective control and took part in its fight against the Japanese invaders. But throughout the Japanese War, the Party concentrated more on consolidating its position with the peasantry and on undermining Chiang Kai-shek's régime than on fighting the Japanese. As soon as the Japanese surrendered to the Americans and British and withdrew from China, the two parties, Communist and Kuomintang, leapt at each other's throat and a bloody civil war began. The communists swept all before them, harnessing the enthusiasm of the peasantry in the fight against reactionaries, and for the great new campaign of land reform.

China is not the only country that has carried out land reform. Many countries in Asia, Africa and Europe have undertaken land reform and many more are planning it. In all these countries there has always been a constant element: the landlords put up a stiff and sometimes protracted resistance before yielding to superior political power and pressure or to clever manoeuvres. It was much the same in China, but with one important difference.

Whereas in most other countries where land reform has been undertaken some form of compensation has been paid, or at least promised, to dispossessed landlords, the Chinese Communist Party got the land for nothing.

Many of the more timid (and more perspicacious landlords), seeing the ease with which the communist armies swept over the country, and fearful of reprisals, promptly packed up their movable belongings and fled with the retreating forces of the Kuomintang. Their land, of course, remained behind. Some craftier landlords (for whom the Chinese term is best rendered as 'vacillators' or 'fence-sitters') cautiously watched the trend of events till they were certain the communists had come to stay, and then declared themselves communist supporters. They saved their lives by the skin of their teeth, but they could not save their land.

A third set of landlords clung tenaciously to their land, some hoping against hope that there would be no, or only slight, retribution, others adopting that attitude of the man who sees his house on fire and says: 'This is all I value and cherish. I will perish with it.' Many preferred to face extinction rather than abandon the homesteads and shrines of their ancestors. .

Led by activists of the Party and those anxious to curry favour with the country's new masters, the peasants murdered most of these landlords. Armed with cudgels, knives and pole-axes, and sometimes with ancient flint-lock guns, the peasants surrounded the landlord's house and forced him out of his lair. To make the whole thing look something less than cold-blooded murder, a mock trial was held in which the landlord was reminded of the number of catties of rice and millet he had stolen from the peasants, the number of peasant women he had raped or forced into concubinage and anything else they could think of. After this he was hanged from his own

C

gate-post or from the nearest tree. So enthusiastic were the peasants in visiting on the landlords the grievances and miseries of centuries that millions were slaughtered at this time.

Away with the Kuomintang, away with the landlords! But everybody did not live happily ever after as in the fairy story.

*   *   *

Land was distributed to all landless peasants. But a basic problem remained. The majority of peasants were so poor that they had not the simplest tools for cultivating the land. Without tools, the newly distributed land was useless to these people. To overcome this difficulty, 'mutual aid teams' were formed, which operated as follows. Four peasant households, each perhaps having 'one leg of cattle', teamed together and became the joint owners of the whole animal. Other peasants owning perhaps mattocks or hoes, or maybe even a plough, joined the team, which as a result had a full set of tools and a draught animal for cultivation. They no longer had to pay for the hire of the tools with the product of their toil. The Party had broken the grip of the landlord and the money-lender. The peasants were free to dispose of their produce as it suited them. What a blessing the Party had wrought for the peasants!

For the peasants, the problem was pretty well solved, but for the Party, not so, not by a long way. The anti-Japanese war and the civil war had been costly and were won only by means of massive Soviet aid. Industrialisation was being undertaken in earnest (also with Soviet aid) and money had to be found, and plenty of it, to pay off war debts and to finance the industrialisation program. Where was the money to come from? In a country like China with a predominantly peasant economy, the answer readily suggested itself: from the peasants.

Make the peasants pay. But first it was necessary to devise an efficient method for taxing the peasantry. In the mutual aid teams, everyone had control over his share of the produce of the team; it was difficult for the Party to be sure that everyone declared his harvest-share correctly. To get over this difficulty, agricultural produce co-operatives were formed under pressure from the Party. To make these co-operatives work, it was necessary that the peasants should surrender the land they had so recently won from the landlords. The land had to be owned in common. The peasants didn't like this, but the Party had by then grown too powerful to yield easily to any pressure. The peasants had no other choice but to surrender.

The co-operatives enabled the state to tax the peasants to some extent, but the Party found the method of taxation still imperfect. So communes were introduced. These communes were intended to be self-contained units, providing for their members, as far as possible, everything that was needed. Each commune contained up to 5,000 households (a household in China may include not only father, mother and children, but also grandparents, grandchildren and assorted cousins). Amongst the activities of a rural commune are agriculture and animal husbandry, forest and water conservation, fisheries, and the construction and operation of factories. Its services include education, care for the aged and all the amenities a self-contained community requires.

The celebrated 'liberation of women' did not spring entirely from an enlightened desire to improve the lot of women. It happened that during the drive for water conservation, so many peasants were drafted to dam-sites that a serious shortage of hands for farm labour was created. To remedy this, women were 'liberated' to join the ranks of labour. This was achieved by compelling everyone to take meals in the communal messes, thus freeing women from cooking and duties, and by establishing nurseries, thus relieving women of the care of their children. The nursery scheme killed three birds with one stone; it ensured that children would be trained from the earliest age in the rudiments of communist doctrine; it undermined the basis of family allegiance; and it freed women for labour.

*   *   *

It was early in the spring of 1961 that I made my first visit to a rural commune. A group of African students—Camerounians, Zanzibaris, Somalis and Ghanaians—were touring southern China and were taken to visit one of the communes on the outskirts of Shanghai. Shanghai, by the way, is China's biggest city and perhaps the biggest or second biggest in Asia. The city authorities told us its population was ten million. It is a little ironic to find the Chinese boasting of the size and imposing grandeur of Shanghai, the city the capitalist Europeans built.

As we drank gallons of commune tea and chain-smoked their cigarettes, the manager of the commune gave us an introductory talk on the set-up of the commune, after which he led a tour round it. Contrary to what the manager had led me to expect, I saw no tractors in the fields. What I saw was a large number of men and women, some transplanting cabbage, others weeding the cabbage patches. They were all working either with their bare hands or with long-handled hoes. When we reached the kindergarten, the toddlers all clapped their tiny hands in welcome, as is the custom of the country. 'Mǐ hǎo

bóbó', they cried! 'How do you do, uncle.' Then they
sang us in their shrill little voices songs in praise of their
father, Mao Tse-tung.

The communal dining hall had four walls and a roof. I
saw no windows, and there did not appear to be any
tables or chairs, or even benches. What I saw was a
large number of chop-bowls and chop-sticks stacked on
the floor along the walls. I wondered at the time whether
they ate their food standing, but as it happened I
didn't ask about this. Adjoining the dining hall was the
kitchen. Several women were busy preparing what we
were told was the communal lunch. A giant cauldron
was simmering over a huge fire. Inside it was cabbage—
the communal lunch.

As we moved from the kitchen to another part of the
commune, the manager pointed towards a shed: 'There
now is one of our tractors.' I followed his finger, but saw
no tractor. What I saw was a green something-or-other
that looked very much like a motor scooter. Could a
tractor really be so tiny? I told the interpreter I would
like the manager to take me to the shed for a closer look.
My request was translated. I am sure the manager
heard and understood it, but when he started to move,
it was not towards the 'tractor', but away from it. So
I never had a chance to verify whether the thing standing
in the shed was a tractor. Still, in those days I was
diffident and hopeful of the best, so I followed him,
swallowing my disbelief.

The buildings in this commune were the same as
those you find everywhere in the Chinese countryside;
houses built of mud and roofed with mud or, sometimes,
with slates and tiles. Here and there new houses were
being built, one-storey adobe affairs.

Before the visit, we had been told a great deal about
the communes and had been led to expect something

tremendous and impressive. We eagerly looked foward
to seeing the Chinese achievement.

Our countries in Africa, like China, were lately freed
from foreign domination. Africa's problems in agriculture and industrialisation must in many points be
closer to China's than to those of highly advanced
countries. By studying China's methods, we hoped to
come across something that could benefit our own
countries. From the accounts we had had of it, the
commune system certainly seemed capable of being as
good for Africa as for China.

Thinking on these lines prompted a companion from
Ghana and I to ask to be allowed to pay a second visit to
this commune near Shanghai. There was some difficulty
in getting this request allowed. The authorities in
Shanghai wanted us to submit beforehand a list of the
questions we wanted to ask the manager of the commune.
I took umbrage at this and played on the fact that the
Chinese are anxious to please foreigners, especially
Africans, whom they want to convert to communism.
After some shilly-shallying, they agreed to let us pay a
special visit. When we returned to the commune three
days after our first visit, we had plenty of time for a
leisurely talk with the manager. He quoted us figures to
prove that the living standard of the peasants was
rising rapidly. He also informed us that the peasants
shared the commune's produce, each receiving according
to his or her contribution in labour. One question I remember pressing on him with some insistence: Did the
peasants, of their own accord, decide to set up the
commune, or did an order come from the Party? His
reply was that the peasants did it 'voluntarily'. I learned
later that this was a bare-faced lie. I think he must
have taken us for a couple of school-children whom he
could fool with fairy tales. By the way, I used the word

'voluntarily' with reluctance because in communist jargon it has a very unpleasant connotation, which I shall explain later.

In China, information from private sources is generally far more reliable than official information. Get into private conversation with a Chinese student or worker (but make sure first he is not a party-member or a Youth Leaguer) who knows you well and trusts you (i.e. knows you are not a spy for the authorities), and he will tell you the truth about anything you put to him in conversation. An official has to be extremely cautious, especially when dealing with foreigners, since a mistake on his part will entail heavy penalties. Thus, the official account as obtained from the manager of this commune near Shanghai in February 1961 was that their fields always yielded bumper harvests and that the peasants' standard of living was steadily rising. Yet that very year, for the third successive year, the food and clothing ration allowances were reduced throughout the whole of China, till the people had barely enough to keep body and soul together. The commune official told us fairy tales; it was the ordinary people who told us of the merciless hunger. Of course, it is quite conceivable that this particular commune could have bumper harvests while other communes or areas suffered failures in the harvest. But in so far as a man's attitude in speaking can lead to a fair assessment of the truth of what he is saying, I found it hard to put much trust in his account.

He said nothing about the proportion of the harvest which is taken away by the state. Only the common people who felt the pangs told us about this. It was they who told us that since the establishment of the communes the quantity of grain and other crops taken by the state as tax from the peasants had been mounting steadily.

The last figures I got in China were as follows: to the state: 70 per cent; to the peasant: 30 per cent.

In obedience to the sacred principle of winning foreign currency, the hungry peasants have to be fleeced to the maximum and their grain shipped to the USSR, Ceylon and elsewhere. Had I studied economics, I would perhaps have understood how it pays China to export large quantities of rice and other foodstuffs to Cuba, Ceylon, Russia and to other countries which have vastly more food and smaller populations by comparison; and while doing this, to import still larger quantities from Canada and Australia. The only explanation I can think of is that China has some outstanding commitments which she considers she has to fulfil despite her own shortage of food, and which her contracting partners are too hard-fisted to forgo in consideration of China's internal plight. If this is the case, it wouldn't surprise me to learn that some of the Canadian and Australian wheat is going to meet those foreign commitments instead of feeding China's hungry masses.

This second visit of mine to the commune, though a great disappointment, was not such a waste of time as it first appeared. Through it I learnt how untrustworthy Chinese officials can be. This knowledge has enabled me many times to keep afloat when I would otherwise have sunk in the troubled sea that is modern China. It also taught me that there is nothing positive (I mean positively good) that Africa can gain from the Chinese type of commune.

*   *   *

I cannot say whether the experiment of the commune, disastrous in China, may not work in other places, at other times and if divorced from the unappealing and sometimes positively inhuman aspects that characterise the Chinese communes.

As a father, I have known no greater joy than to hold my child and tell myself: 'This is my own child; my own flesh and blood.' I have a friend, a very dear friend, whose father was a coal miner. When his son was born, the collier resolved that his son should never be a miner, but have a better lot in life. That man drudged and slaved to give his son that good education which alone could give him an opening to something better than working in the mines.

Tell me an aim, please, more worthy, more noble than that of this loving father.

Human beings are basically the same, no matter what their race, or colour, or station in life, or environment. How could the Chinese mother or father have welcomed a system that required their baby to be taken away to a nursery to be reared and bred to a state blueprint? Because of long working hours, an overcrowded working week, and the sessions of political education that are compulsory at the end of each day's work, parents had very little chance of meeting their children. And that is just what the state intended. Children are to be prevented from picking up any individualistic notions from their natural parents; all their ideas must come from their foster parent, the state.

If progress means that every attempt shall be made to sever the natural loyalties of the family; if progress means that children shall be made to love an abstract state more than they love their parents; if progress means putting an official ban on mutual and natural love and its expression in man and woman: then keep such progress to yourself; don't foist it off on me.

The miser who hoards up everything he can lay hands on is an extreme case. The religious ascetic who gives up all his earthly possessions to follow the call of God is an extreme case also. In between these extremes lies the great mass of humanity who for countless generations have labelled some things 'private': 'mine' as opposed to 'ours'. Certainly the six hundred million Chinese must be an extraordinary aberration from normality if, while sane and sober, they could decide to hand over to the state, not only their private property (land, huts, hens, cattle, pots and pans, everything), but also their children. The Chinese Communist Party would have us believe that they did so decide and did it 'voluntarily'.

I am now very suspicious of people who use this word 'voluntary', even when it is spoken in good faith. It is employed with an unpleasant connotation in some parts of the world, not only in China. And I'm sorry to say that Africa is not immune from hypocritical and cynical use of the word. Not so long ago the Trade Union Congress of my own country felt the need to raise union dues from two shillings a month to four shillings. The order for the increase came from the very top (the Trade Union Congress in Ghana is controlled by the government), and union officials promptly drafted resolutions on behalf of the workers urging an increase in the monthly dues. The first the workers heard of the increase was when they saw in the newspapers that they had 'voluntarily' asked for it. Meekly they paid the increase until political trouble flared up and the question of the increased dues got mixed up with politics, and the President himself had to make a statement. He feigned that he had not known of the matter at all and indeed thought the dues were too high! The dues were reduced to their former level. But all this happened at a time when the ruling circles in Ghana had not mastered fully the implications and applications of the term 'voluntary'.

To make a man do something 'voluntarily', you must first make him understand the implications of his not doing it: the ration tickets that may not be forthcoming; the people higher up who are going to be displeased, and so on and so forth. That's how to do it; that's the Chinese style. And in China I saw so many people do so many things 'voluntarily' that voluntary demonstrations of solidarity in Ghana are just child's play. China's imitators in Africa, after some initial blunders, are now proving quite competent in this 'voluntary' game.

But 'voluntaryism' in the end has not saved the communes. They didn't work. They made the serious food situation worse, not better, for peasants had no incentive to work harder and produce more and more of less and less for themselves. Docile as they are, the Chinese people could be driven like the proverbial horse to water, but not made to drink. The people's communes have disintegrated, for the present at least. Children are now back with their parents. The Party now permits peasants to own a few pigs and chickens and such other small domestic animals as they can afford.

Has the Party learned its lesson? One hopes so. But it is likely that the grip it sought to exercise over the peasants by means of the communes will be maintained in other ways.

5

Two Feet of Cloth

It gives me no pleasure to describe the wretched state of affairs in China. The country is in a parlous condition by any standards, and to gloat over it would be despicable. But the facts of the situation should be made known. China's sole reason for keeping the facts hidden from the rest of the world is based on the realisation that making them known to others would be tantamount to admitting her own and communism's failure. Such an admission would seriously jeopardise her chances of wooing the new nations, particularly those in Africa. So China elects to suffer in silence: a self-imposed silence.

One might ask whether such people really deserve anyone's sympathy. My answer to this is yes and no. Whatever the case, it is always necessary to bear in mind that there are two different elements involved: the Party, and the people. It is the Party (with a membership of about sixteen million) which introduced the communes for the purpose of controlling and fleecing six hundred million people. It is the Party that, each successive year, appealed to the people to tighten their belts while communist officials loosened theirs to enjoy the fruits of exploitation. It is the Party that has obstinately refused to appeal to the world for help for fear of damaging the cause of global communism. On such a Party I can waste no sympathy; maybe you can? But to the suffering masses of China the world needs a thought. It is they who are being pushed along a road which they have no wish to travel. For them I have a deep and angry sympathy.

Foodstuffs are strictly rationed and the quota allowed appears barely enough to keep life going. I say 'appears' because I judge from the quantity and quality of the food alone and not from any scientific calculation of the ration's calorific content. The bulk of the people's food, as I have already stated, is made up of cabbage. If people so dote on cabbage that they make it almost their sole item of diet, I won't quarrel with their taste, though a dietician might have plenty to say about it. But I certainly quarrel with the wisdom and intentions of a government that will reduce a whole people to a diet of cabbage against its will. Cabbage has always had a part in the diet in parts of China; but I doubt if the man-in-the-street in China would have believed it if told in 1948 that, after the glorious liberation, the inspired leadership of the Communist Party would reduce him to growing four cabbage crops a year in order to subsist.

Because of the scarcity of rice the people fall back, where possible, on sweet potatoes and *wŏ tóu*, a kind of steamed bread made of maize flour. The morning meal usually consists of a bowl of very watery rice-gruel; the midday meal of white cabbage and a ball of maize bread as big as my fist (and I have not got a large hand); and the evening meal of more white cabbage and another piece of *wŏ tóu*. In cooking, the emphasis is on bulk rather than on delicacy. The average man doesn't eat meat, fish or eggs, not because he doesn't like them, but because he just can't get them. It is only people of a recognised standing with the Party who have a chance to get their teeth into food of this sort; people like the President of the Language Institute who has an allowance of fifteen kilograms of meat each month for himself and his family.

Food tickets are issued which are valid for a certain locality only. Travelling to other localities without official permission pretty nearly amounts to attempted suicide since, without special arrangements with the authorities permitting the journey, there is no food for you when you get there. One of my teachers told me that he often felt he would like to visit friends in another part of Peking, but had found visits of such a distance impossible because they would mean missing his midday meal and supper at the school. He took it for granted that his friends would have nothing to spare for him when he got there.

Many of the Chinese students told me that they had not eaten meat for about three years, nor had they been luckier with milk and eggs. There was a time, they said, when a student who could afford it could eat meat; but things had changed drastically with the introduction of the communes. Even money will not get you food if the authorities say you shall not have it.

There are, it is true, some items of food which are still unrationed, though I'm not sure if they can be properly classified as foodstuff in the accepted sense. I mean wild vegetables. Previous famines in their history have prompted the Chinese to make many adventurous gastronomic experiments, with the result that they know of a large number of wild, edible herbs, weeds and grasses, which are all grouped under the general term of 'wild vegetables'. Many of these can lend variety to a meal, and as additions to the diet they have an appreciable nutritional value. But they cannot be considered as adequate substitutes for cereals, meat and eggs.

In my language textbook there were many stories which related that some people in pre-liberation days were so poor that they lived exclusively on wild vegetables and the food they managed to steal from other people. But, so the stories ran, food became plentiful after the liberation thanks to the Party's correct leadership, and everyone now could live happily on a full stomach. We were put to reading these stories at the very time when we could see from our classroom windows, not 200 yards away, children and adults alike picking about for wild vegetables. I saw this sort of thing happening with my own eyes in many different places, but usually in the fields on the western side of our Institute. Yet the Party would have us foreigners believe that all was well with everyone, even down to the little boy who volunteered the information that he hadn't enough to eat and what there was did not make good eating.

Foreign students get preferential treatment; in the same college where the Chinese students had not had milk for well nigh three years, I, or any other foreign student, could have a bottle of milk every morning, also pork, beef, mutton or fish—and all because the Party thinks that, by treating us well, we can be bamboozled into accepting communism and implanting it in our own countries. The contrast between this special treatment meted out to us and the grim situation for the Chinese students became more and more painful.

At the beginning of 1961, Chinese students were spending about 10 yuan (roughly thirty shillings) on food each month. The food is very cheap; cabbage is never very costly anywhere in the world. But by the time I left Peking, in April 1962, students in the Medical College were spending an average of only 5 yuan each month on food. The situation had grown so bad that even rice, which used to be the commonest item of food, had become unavailable. The Chinese students had not tasted rice for the three months preceding my departure.

I remember a student in the Language Institute bitterly complaining about the fifteen kilograms of meat that was the monthly quota of the Institute's President. I agreed that he had every right to complain. The President was an old man to whom meat and other protein foods are no longer as important as they are to a growing student. But in China such considerations do not matter. The President was a senior member of the Party; the student was not. Of course, it may well be the President had young children in his family and the fifteen kilograms of meat went to them. But the fathers of students also had young children in *their* families. In 'egalitarian socialist' China, it all depends on whose family you belong to whether or not you get meat.

In the winter of 1961–2, the Chinese students of the Eastern compound of the Language Institute were reduced to what was pretty well a begging racket. One evening as I hurried with a foreign companion through the snow from the foreigners' dining hall towards my dormitory in Block 4, we were accosted by a Chinese student lurking in a dark corner. He told us he had lost all his food tickets three days before and as a result had not been able to eat for three days. I should perhaps pause here to make it clear that the food ticket does not guarantee free food; it authorises you to buy an allotted quantity of food per meal. You will starve to death if you have money but no food tickets. A good many Africans I have spoken to are under the delusion that socialism means free food, free houses, free almost everything. It does not mean this in China or, as far as I can see, in any other country where socialism is being practised: Ghana for example.

Well, the poor fellow's tone was so piteous we just could not ignore him. While I stayed talking with him, my companion went back to the foreign students' mess to see what he could get. Supper was pretty well over and done with and all he could get was five balls of *mán tóu*, a kind of steamed wheaten bread. We took him to our dormitory and gave him the *mán tóu* and a cup of hot ovaltine, promising to let him have similar supplies every evening until the end of the month when he would be able to obtain new food tickets. He stuffed his stomach and then his pockets with the *mán tóu*, and then made elaborate arrangements for a rendezvous at a lonely spot on the playground where there was no chance of his being seen taking food from us. He would be severely 'criticised', he said, if the transaction were known by other comrades. After repeated promises of secrecy on our part, he left us. Days afterwards I learned from other foreign students that they had had similar experiences. Begging for food on a winter's night became a regular thing. And who could blame those poor Chinese students whom hunger had driven to acts of which they would normally be ashamed?

'Next Sunday I shall come so that we play'; so said a student in the Spanish department whose business it was to spy on me (every foreign student has one or several of these spies attached to him). I should explain that the Chinese word *wánr* can be translated as 'play', 'enjoy oneself', 'go for a walk', and so on, according to the circumstances; but Chinese studying foreign languages generally use the most literal translation, 'play'. He came that Sunday, and all he did was to suggest that we should have some food and drink to 'play' with. From the foreign students' dining hall I brought him a huge plate-ful of rice and stew and a bottle of beer. After making sure that the door was locked, he ate his fill. After several successive Sundays of this kind of one-sided 'play', I had to put my foot down and make him understand

that my conception of 'play' was rather different. I was
going broke in this wonderful new kind of play.

*   *   *

Even the coarse blue cotton cloth everyone dresses in has
become so scarce that each person's quota for the year is
limited to two feet. By this I mean that the length of
cloth an average Chinese can buy in any one year is two
feet of twenty-four inches. The usual breadth of cloth
in China is three feet. No more. There is no mistake about
this. The Chinese word for foot (as a measurement) is
chǐ. The term for metre is *gōng chǐ*. The annual cloth
ration as I knew it was clearly defined as *liǎng chǐ*, i.e.
two feet, not two metres.

One can buy six inches of four different kinds of cloth
or one foot of two different kinds. Everyone is supplied
with cloth coupons for two feet of cloth, and that amount
cannot be exceeded. To buy a new pair of trousers, it is
necessary to save up coupons for two years or more. In
most cases people prefer to use their cloth ration to
patch up their old clothes. The precious ration cannot be
wasted on such fripperies as handkerchiefs, and this
contributes to perpetuating the unpleasant habit of
spitting everywhere and anywhere.

The two feet of cloth business brought to light some
new and rather surprising habits among the girls. In the
International Club one Saturday I saw a pretty girl in
flowing red skirt dancing with a foreigner. This Club,
by the way, is the only one in Peking and is run mainly
for foreign diplomats and visitors. Students are not
normally allowed in. When the dance ended, this girl
came over in my direction to sit down. Imagine my
surprise when, before settling in her seat, she raised the
whole of the bottom of her skirt and sat down plump on

her drawers! But this was just a demonstration of Chinese home economy. With her two feet of cloth a year she could buy a new pair of drawers, but not a new flowing skirt. It is therefore better to wear out the drawers than to wear out the skirt. Can you beat that?

State factories and commercial houses have also joined in the economy campaign in the best socialist style. When I wanted to buy an alarm clock in February 1962, I heard the same monotonous chant of *méi yŏu* (not available) wherever I went. It was not until mid-March that I was able to buy a clock. Because there is never enough of anything, state factories and shops have to wait for weeks—often for months—before they can stockpile enough of a particular commodity for release onto the market. Salesmen join in the game by disposing of a fixed quantity of a given article each day. After the day's quota has been sold out, all the would-be customers get *méi yŏu* until the next day. Even the central post office of the People's Republic of China sometimes runs short of air mail letter cards and everybody has to wait patiently until the factory concerned releases its stockpile.

Bicycles and watches (particularly wrist-watches) are very scarce. When new supplies become available, party-members have a right of pre-emption. Students are not permitted to buy wrist-watches.

Despite the serious tobacco shortage, a surprisingly large number of Chinese still remain smokers. All tobacco and all imitation tobacco are rationed. By imitation tobacco I mean stuff made from leaves of some kind which so far as I could make out have no relation whatever to the tobacco plant. It is an evil-smelling concoction. The normal ration of each worker per month is between twenty and forty sticks, depending on the individual's status. Party-members are allowed more and

of better quality. Foreigners, like the high mandarins of
the Party, can smoke unlimited quantities of the best
brands. When things reach this stage, the fitting term
for it is not 'austerity in adversity', but 'exploitation'.

6

Exploitation of Man by State

'Capitalism means exploitation of man by man.' 'In socialist countries there is no exploitation.' We have heard these phrases so often that we tend to assume automatically that they are true. The first statement may be true; the second is utterly false.

In China I witnessed mass exploitation on a scale much vaster than the capitalists at their worst have ever been able to attain, much less surpass. It was not long after my arrival in Peking that I found out about the exploitation. It all started with an electric pressing iron.

After a few weeks in Peking, I found that all my white shirts that had been to the laundry had turned an unsightly yellow hue. Chinese laundrymen in communist China do not seem to take the same pride in their work as most Chinese laundrymen do when they set up shop abroad. I decided to do my own laundering. So, one Saturday afternoon I went to the 'Great House of a Hundred Wares', the big department store in Peking, and bought an electric pressing iron. It was a very simple affair, not at all like the kind of streamlined article offered by the 'exploiting capitalists'; but it was an iron all right, and that was what I wanted. I felt lucky to get one. They are so scarce, and those that can be got are so unreliable that most Chinese do not iron their clothes. On New Year's Eve, 1960, I saw a group of about fifty Chinese students troop onto the stage at the Language

Institute to sing. Boys and girls all wore white shirts, but not a single shirt was ironed.

I used the iron that very night to press my clothes. But next morning the thing absolutely refused to heat again. I took it to a member of the staff, complaining bitterly over the lost 17 yuan (about fifty shillings) I had spent on it. He said he would repair it, but after fiddling about with it for a week, he returned it in no better condition. I was irritated at the idea of having my money thrown down the drain, so off I went with the iron to the department store and asked for a new one. The man at the counter argued that, since I had allowed someone to fiddle with it, there was nothing he could do about it. That was a fair point; so, following his advice, I bought a new heating element for about 3 yuan (roughly nine shillings) and sent the iron to an electrical repair shop he recommended. It was repaired, but after working for just one day, it went bust again. When I learnt at the repair shop that the new heating element had burned out, I grew so furious that I took the whole contraption back to the department store and told the assistant the state could have it as a gift. I couldn't speak enough Chinese then, but I had my speech written out on paper at the school.

Another time I bought a badminton racquet and a box of shuttlecocks for 15 yuan (about forty-five shillings). The racquet was a beautiful affair with green polythene strings and a slender metal handle. But to my utter disgust it could carry me through only three games. The shuttlecocks did not last five minutes each. I sent these back to the store with a letter saying they were a gift to the state and that I should think twice before buying Chinese goods again. Several months afterwards, the manager of the department store came to see me at the Institute to apologise. 'The factories have no experience', he pleaded. The full cost of all the articles I returned as 'gifts to the state' was refunded me.

Now this is the main point of my argument. A capitalist employs, say, 100 men, and produces, say, a million articles which he passes on to the consuming public. That capitalist, before going into production, may have spent thousands or perhaps hundreds of thousands of pounds in experimenting to find out the best way of making his article more acceptable to the public, and how to produce it most cheaply. After he is ready with his prototype, state organisations (the National Physical Laboratory in Britain, the National Bureau of Standards in the United States) arc on the look-out to see that he does not cheat the public by passing worthless products off on them. It is only after this prototype has passed strict tests that the capitalist can proceed with mass production.

Moreover, and what is more important, market competition in capitalist countries is so keen and consumers so very discriminating that generally the capitalist has to take care that his products are of good quality.

But what did I see in China? State factories turn out articles with almost no thought to the consumers' tastes. The public is expected to put up with what the state factories turn out. A state factory employing, say, 100 workers, turns out a million goods not worth their value. Because of lack of competition, little attempt is made to improve quality. The range and variety of products is also very limited. In very many cases, these articles, as I found out for myself, are priced much higher than their equivalent in the capitalist world. Assuming, for argument's sake, that the communist state factory pays a fair wage to its 100 workers, it is nevertheless passing on shoddy articles to the consumer and this represents cheating the public to an extent which my hypothetical capitalist could not manage.

This is exploitation. And when one considers that, in
fact, very low wages are earned in China, it is shocking
exploitation. Tutors in the Foreign Language Institute
earn 40 yuan (about £6 a month); the dean of the foreign
students' department earns 100 yuan (about £15 a month)
while the foreign students under him receive allowances
of between 100 and 150 yuan. China has a trade union:
the All-China Federation of Trade Unions; but this body
has no bargaining power on behalf of the workers. It only
organises the workers into groupings so that they can be
more effectively controlled and exploited by the state.
Another form of the same exploitation is the example I
cited earlier of the state's whizzling 70 per cent of their
farm produce from the peasants.

If this is not exploitation, then what in heaven's name
is? I fully accept that there are unscrupulous and mean
capitalists, but can what they do compare with what goes
on in a country where the state itself has become one
vast unscrupulous exploiter?

Citizens of a country seeking to industrialise itself need
certainly to make some patriotic sacrifices. But the common citizens reasonably can demand patriotism from the
state and from national manufacturers. They can rightly
insist that these establishments sacrifice some time and
money and some mental effort in research and re-
organisation to improve their products. If that is patriotism, I certainly wouldn't object to smoking cheap
locally produced cigarettes for some time. But it is
asking too much to expect me to continue my sacrifices indefinitely when my country's manufacturers
utterly ignore the consumer by refusing to make improvements in manufacturing methods and in the
finished product.

Chinese bicycles sell in China for between 200 and 300

yuan (£30 to £40), but when exported they sell at only 85 yuan, or about £12. This seems incredible, but the fact is that Chinese bicycles cannot compete in sturdiness and finish with foreign bicycles, so their price has to be reduced almost to dumping-rates. In China, where there is no competition, the state factories can sell their machines at any price. I have seen Chinese ready to pay 300 yuan for an old Raleigh bicycle rather than spend the same amount on a brand new bicycle made in China. (In many parts of West Africa, *new* Raleigh and other British bicycles sell at around £17, which in Chinese money is about 120 yuan.)

I remember also having seen a Chinese buy for 200 yuan (almost £30) a watch that did not cost £5 in Hong Kong where it was made, even though Chinese watches were available for the equivalent of £11 10*s*. Chinese, even communist Chinese, can be quality-conscious to the extent of discriminating against their own in favour of foreign goods, if given the chance, and even when these foreign, capitalist products reach them at inflated black market prices. I don't imagine that the manufacturers of Raleigh bicycles and Omega watches have much chance of conducting a sales-drive in China, but at least it must be some satisfaction to them to know that their products command such high respect in that country that people are willing to pay extravagantly high prices for them.

*   *   *

My travelling companion on the Trans-Siberian railway in April 1962 was an amiable young Russian. He had brought from Peking two big trunk-loads of woollen sweaters and other clothing. He was going to sell them when he arrived in Moscow (this citizen of socialist

Russia: could he possibly have been engaging in capitalist activities? Surely not; we are told there are no private capitalists in socialist countries; of course, we must believe what we are told!). He was taking all these clothes away from Peking, the same city where, not quite two months before, Chinese workers and students were imploring me and other foreigners to help them obtain warm winter clothing.

During that winter, I went to the 'Great House of a Hundred Wares' to buy some thick woollen material for lining my windcheater. I got what I wanted. But when the next man in the queue—a Chinese worker— asked to buy some of the same material, he got the *méi yŏu* treatment. Though the bale of cloth was lying right in front of him, it was 'unavailable'.

Chinese socialism is supposed to have been introduced for the benefit of the Chinese masses, the people so mercilessly exploited by the landlord class in the old China. But whom was this socialism benefiting in the instances I cite? The Russian foreigner, intent on making a private deal for his own profit; me, the African foreigner whom the Chinese want to convert to communism.

I was friend to a whole family living in a suburb of Peking; five men, seven women, and five children, including baby twins. They had some inducement to cherish my friendship for on every visit I took them sausages, beef, cigarettes and sweets. Their compound consisted of three little huts and a kitchen, all built of mud. Each room had a large bed of baked mud with a big hole beneath it. In better days this hole had held glowing embers to warm the occupants of the bed during the long winter nights. Now they huddle, four and five to a bed, over cavernous holes which generate no warmth because there is no fuel. In winter the drinking water in the earthenware pots in the bedrooms often froze solid. The huts offered next to no protection from the biting north wind: doors and windows were all of plaited grass. Thanks to the sweaters bought by me with their money, at least two members of that family now have something warm to wear in winter. They had money for warm clothes, It was just that these were 'not available' to them. I, the foreigner, could have pretty well anything I liked.

In this land where men once froze with cold because they had no money to buy clothes, they now freeze with cold because there are no clothes to be bought with their money. What difference does it really make to a man whether he freezes with the blessing of communist Mao Tse-tung or reactionary Chiang Kai-shek? He freezes either way. And my friends and innumerable other families were still freezing after twelve years of communist promises. They were still freezing at the time when China could afford to equip, with the people's money, a large army to invade India.

The capitalist exploits the labour of his employees; the lion's share of the proceeds he uses as it suits his pleasure. This is judged unpardonable. Seventy per cent of the peasant's harvest goes to the socialist state. But this is pardonable. Yes, but only if the state provides for the needs of the people from the proceeds of its exactions.

What do the people need? Food to eat, clothes to wear, houses to live in, security in old age: all those things which, properly used, make for human happiness.

But what does the Party want? World prestige, bombs, more territory, propaganda to convert Africa, Southeast Asia and Latin America to communism: all those things which, left to themselves, the Chinese masses would least want to have.

What do the people get? What the Party wants. The

Party is mighty, so its wishes hold sway. In place of more rice, the people have more bombs.

I am told that this is not exploitation. I don't know whether you are still in the mood to repeat the bogus slogan about the absence of exploitation under socialism. I am not; not now. And just by the way: if you happen to go to China on a delegation, let it drop casually that you are rather tired of your watch. You are certain to catch some communist boss in the very uncommunist act of offering you an exorbitant price for it. Only you must expect the business to be transacted behind carefully closed doors.

*   *   *

In some of his later prefaces to the Communist Manifesto, Engels frankly admitted that some of the hideous conditions which prompted the writing of that document in defence of the workers had changed somewhat. It was a good many years since that change started. Today the worker in the capitalist world enjoys such a wide measure of rights and benefits that Marx and Engels, if they were to come back to earth again, would hardly recognise in modern capitalism the successor to the evil system they knew. Trade unions, hardly known in their day, and impotent where they did exist, now protect workers, and few employers now dare make their employees work under unhygienic or inhuman conditions. Workers refuse to work when they consider their wages inadequate or when they are maltreated in any way. In this they have the full support and backing of the unions, now become very powerful organisations.

In the communist system, by contrast, workers have no say over their wages and working conditions. The trade unions in communist countries are organisations whose job is to bring the workers together for more efficient exploitation by the state. What is more, these unions, which should be the guardians and protectors of the workers, do all they can to ensure that the workers shall not complain about poor working conditions. With regard to workers' welfare, is communism marching forward or backward?

I have often heard the pro-communist argument put forward that, since in communist countries all the means of production belong to 'the people', it is nonsensical for workers to strike against themselves, and that therefore strikes are out of place in 'socialist states'. But since working conditions in communist countries are still far off from the supposed ideal, it follows that there are still great improvements to be made. If the right to decide on and to implement such improvements belonged entirely and in fact to 'the people', all that they seek would have been worked for and achieved long ago. But the case is not so. What 'the people' shall have is determined by the state, which is the same as saying that it is determined by the Party. So the people are still left with a vast amount of things to complain about, but they are now without the instruments (petitions, negotiations, demonstrations, strikes) with which to make and enforce their demands.

With the poor food, poor housing, poor wages and poor almost everything that I saw in China, and with the state spending vast sums on armaments and propaganda campaigns to communise other countries, how can anyone honestly argue that the means of production, and consequently the fruits of their labour, belong to the Chinese people?

I am sure that if Marx and Engels could see from another world, call it heaven or hell as you like, the hypocritical actions of those who call themselves communists, they would weep a whole Pacific of tears over the use and abuse to which their theories have been put.

I remember reading once, I think it was in the *Reader's Digest*, of a ship's captain who addressed his new crew as follows: 'This ship does not belong to me, it does not belong to you; it belongs to us.' To which one very unsailorly sailor promptly replied: 'Good, let's sell it.' There is no doubt that the captain would not have sold the ship even if the rest of the crew had unanimously voted to sell out and turn landlubbers. He was simply pointing out to his underlings that, for the ship to fare well, officers and men alike must co-operate. Beyond that he never meant a word of what he said. Communist régimes, in a way, are very much like this captain. What they tell their people and the world, the promises they make, are 'just a way of speaking'. Beyond that, their promises to 'the people' hardly mean a thing.

Exploitation of man by man may have been abolished in Red China; but in its place they have exploitation of man by the state. *That* is Chinese socialism.

7

Why Things Went Wrong

I don't very much hold with the opinions of those people, particularly rather conceited politicians, who think that the opinion of the non-expert, in other words, the 'ordinary man', is not of much account. I am no expert on Chinese political and economic affairs, nor on those of any country for that matter, but this does not discourage me from forming my own opinions. Anyone is as free to disagree with my views as I am to air them.

I think three major factors have led to China's present plight: *first*, a myopic agricultural policy, *secondly*, the over-taxing of the peasants; and *thirdly*, a frantic haste to industrialise, partly for internal economic reasons, but partly also to impress the world, and the consequent excessive emphasis on heavy industry to the neglect and detriment of other sectors of national development.

Many countries in Africa and Asia and Latin America still manage to support their populations with only peasant farming. But a country like China with six or maybe even seven hundred million mouths to fill has a much bigger problem, and a radical approach to agriculture is necessary to raise the people from indigence. To feed, clothe and control such a vast, unwieldy population is the biggest single task facing the Chinese government.

'The Communist Party has come; as in the Soviet

Union, tractors will do our ploughing.' So goes the
peasant ditty I read in one of their 'comic' books. But of
these tractors which are supposed to be doing the
ploughing, all I saw was the scooter-like contraption at
the commune near Shanghai (and I suspect it was no
such thing), and a reaper in a small wheat-field in one of
the suburbs of Peking. (There is almost as much cultivation in the suburbs of the cities as in the rural areas
proper. Even the unpaved boulevards in the central
areas of cities have been converted to growing wheat or
cabbage.) No doubt if I had gone on the usual grand tour
arranged for foreign visitors, I would have seen quite
a number of tractors in 'model' communes and farms.
But, except on only one of three occasions, I travelled
unaccompanied on journeys totalling possibly 10,000
miles through endless miles of cultivated fields and in
the most favourable seasons for seeing tractors. In the
spring of 1961 I went from Peking through Tientsin,
Nanking and Shanghai to Hanchow and back again,
when ploughing was in full swing. In August of the
same year, at harvest time, I journeyed from Peking
through Tientsin, Chinhsien and Mukden to the Yalu
river on the Sino-Korean border, and back again; and
then in April 1962, I departed from China on a journey
which took me across country to Manchouli on the Sino-
Soviet border. I travelled through nine provinces in all
(by rail, not by air), and I do not see how I could possibly
have missed the tractors if they were there in the
numbers proclaimed by the Party in its propaganda.

What I did observe were enormous numbers of people
at work in the fields. The Chinese set great store by
sheer numbers. It is the Party's pride to talk of the
five hundred million pairs of hands forming the country's
peasantry, the *nóng mín*. This is why they will send more
men—students and factory workers—to the fields rather

than manufacture more agricultural implements to do the work faster and more efficiently. The materials for making tractors and farming implements are available all right, but the caterpillar treads and the machine-parts go to the army tanks instead. China could solve her hunger problem within two or three years if she could use her tanks for pulling ploughs and reaping machines. But tanks are too precious to be used for anything save a possible attack on Taiwan, so the hunger continues unabated.

Upstream from Nanking, on the banks of the majestic river Yangtse, there stands a chemical fertiliser factory. There may be many more, but evidence of their existence is sadly lacking, for on this front also the Party has chosen to rely mainly on 'man-power'. I never saw chemical fertilisers in use anywhere, but I did see peasants and students using compost made up of cattle dung, human faeces and sometimes, but more rarely, vegetable matter. The contents of all septic tanks are emptied into mule-carts and hauled to the countryside where they are deposited in pits and left to decompose for some time. At tilling time, the stuff is dug up and ploughed into the soil. In the absence of chemical fertilisers, the peasants make very good use of all the materials at their disposal. In the fields along the railway tracks, children and adults alike can often be seen squatting in full view, patriotically fertilising the land. However, though the diet of the people (mainly roughage) makes them good suppliers of natural fertiliser, the land is vast and there is a limit to what even seven hundred million bowels can produce. This is where artificial fertiliser should come in. But no; Quemoy and Matsu must be bombarded, so chemicals go into shells and bombs rather than into the soil.

D

Because of primitive methods and the lack of mechanical aids to cultivation, the peasants are not able to produce enough. And of what they do produce, the state takes away 70 per cent. But by gross miscalculation, the state is cheating itself in cheating the people. Take away 70 per cent of his produce, and the peasant grows disgruntled; with no incentive to greater production, his work slackens; so next year there is less grain both for state and peasants. And so it goes on. That is the simple economics of the matter. Then reckon up the human physical consequences: less calories, and so less energy output and less resistance to disease, all of which leads to heavier and heavier burdens on the already impoverished state in respect to medical services.

                    *   *   *

The Party's disastrous agricultural policy has been influenced to a great extent by the 'Great Leap Forward' in industry. The peasant is the milch-cow for nourishing China's industrial expansion. The Party asserts that China will 'catch up with Britain in fifteen years, particularly in steel production'. This is a bold assertion. But isn't it a little unrealistic? The Chinese forget that British industry is broadly based and is not exclusively concerned with steel production. It took the British many generations to reach their present stage of industrialisation; the Chinese would do the same in a decade and a half. Admittedly, a nation following an already beaten path need not take as much time or work by trial and error so much as did the pioneers who cleared the path. That is why we in Africa, for example, have been able within the space of a century to reach levels which, modest as they are, it would have taken us centuries to reach if left to our own unaided efforts. And in rising beyond our present level, we have the great advantage of being able to learn from the lessons of other people who had an earlier start than us. In our just struggle against the evils of colonialism, intelligent Africans cannot deny that our continent's close association with foreigners during the colonial period has had some beneficial consequences. Most of the great nations of today, in fact, the United States, Britain, France, Russia, and so on got their starting civilisation through the 'intervention' of foreign influences. The point I am making here is simply that there are very few examples recorded in history of a people's pulling itself up by its own bootstraps wholly unaided.

The Chinese forget, moreover, that modern British industry, being part of a democratic society, has been directly concerned with the material welfare of the people, and that this welfare in return has helped in no small measure to stimulate industrial advance. *Das Kapital* still remains their authority on European capitalism and China's communists positively refuse to allow for the fact that substantial changes have taken place in the industrial societies of the West. It is this mistake of regarding their citizens rather as old-style capitalists regarded their workers, *i.e.* as mere human tools and not as individuals with a right to a decent life, that is costing the Chinese so dear and slowing down the progress they are seeking to speed up. Because the Party started by riding roughshod over the peasants in favour of heavy industry, the people's first enthusiasm turned sour and the will to work slackened. When it was almost too late, and the enormity of the food problem hit them hard, the Party began to draft factory workers to the farms with feverish haste, leaving the factories running on only one leg, with consequent detriment to the great leap forward.

We in Africa have ahead of us a task of industrialisation much heavier than that confronting the Chinese. After all, China has for centuries had a highly educated élite and large numbers of people with skills which, even if non-industrial, are capable of adjustment to the demands of industry. And industrialisation of a sort was being introduced into China by foreigners from the beginning of the century. I first clearly realised this when visiting Shanghai. Almost every factory or establishment we visited there had been set up, either by Chinese entrepreneurs or by foreigners before and during the Japanese occupation. The Japanese undertook considerable measures of industrialisation; although the factories they set up operated mainly as assembly plants and not as full-scale factories manufacturing the whole product-range from start to finish, nevertheless the people working in them learned a great deal about industrial techniques. They had an easier task in converting to full-scale industry than that of most African countries whose colonial masters did not even start up assembly plants.

I do not say this to detract from China's achievements. She did indeed take some notable steps forward until the double blow of internal calamity and the withdrawal of Soviet technical assistance crippled her industrial development.

An important lesson for Africa to learn from China is the folly of the craze for prestige for its own sake. A luxury hotel in an African capital is a good thing; it makes the city more attractive to visitors from abroad, and of course (and this is what weighs most with some of our misguided politicians and rulers) it lends prestige. But should mere prestige take precedence over the needs of our people? The money sunk into building and maintaining that plushy hotel could have built clinics, or better housing, or an improved water supply. The same eager chase after prestige leads the new African states to maintain strings of costly embassies all over the world. International affairs are very important, but there is a limit to what a newly emerging country can afford to spend on impressive embassies. I question the wisdom of leaders who leave their countries in poverty and disorder in order to concentrate on international affairs just because they get greater prestige in the world thereby.

Quite frankly, Africa today stands in dire need of a reorientation of thought and a reassessment of values; otherwise things will always go wrong with us, and we cannot keep on for ever blaming the 'imperialists' for all the ills we suffer from. Some at least are of our own making.

As I have said earlier, I do not believe that any political system can be so bad as to be absolutely bad. For example, bad as it is, the Chinese communist régime has helped the people to develop a spirit which seems to be inherent in Chinese nature, the 'do-it-yourself' spirit. Such a spirit could be of incalculable benefit to us Africans. The fact that many of China's 'do-it-yourself' projects have ended in utter failure due to bad planning does not detract from the wholesomeness of that spirit. Something very like it, the pioneering spirit, contributed to America's greatness. Though the Party never admits to its mistakes (it is supposed to be infallible), they have been learning from them. Because the spirit remains even when the plans go wrong, China will sooner or later grow great. A great China with a great population and an outsize bellicosity— a truly terrible China!

If when you visit Peking, you find the city's streets free of litter, do not put this down to good hygienic habits alone; give ninety-nine per cent of the credit to domestic economy. In China waste paper is money. There are special state employees who buy waste paper, whole or broken bottles and glass, old food tins and every imaginable species of scrap. Every rubbish heap has its own detachment of very ancient women assiduously poking in the rubbish, scavenging for waste paper and other scraps.

We in Africa could also do with some domestic economy. If we could waste less, we would be saved a lot of the humiliation we suffer each time we send our ministers and officials abroad on begging tours.

Unemployment: what African state is free from this headache? There is little unemployment in China; can we copy China here? In 1961 a Ghanaian friend and I approached the Vice-Secretary of the Peking Students' Union: we wanted to learn something about the deployment of labour in China. Our request was transmitted to the Labour Ministry which deputised one of its officials to come and talk with us. Unfortunately we found from his talk nothing spectacular about their labour system. What was spectacular was precisely what he did not say, but which we knew for certain from other sources.

When a man needs employment, he registers with the Labour Ministry. If there is no immediate vacancy in his trade or speciality, he may be put to work where the state needs more hands at the given moment. During my stay in China, the unemployed were usually carted off to work on the land. There is much to be said for such a system; but, like most Chinese measures, it ignores the human element.

How I do wish the President of my country had picked only the Chinese grain and thrown away the chaff!

8

Chinese 'Democracy'

Since my school days, I have always accepted democracy as 'government of the people, by the people, for the people'. Though I did not tie myself to the American form as the one and only ideal, I found this definition of Lincoln's summed up what democracy should mean. It was only when I went to China that I started to take that definition apart and re-examine it in the light of my new knowledge. I did not question the logic of accepting Lincoln's definition as the starting point for my analysis, because so far as I could tell, both West and East accept it as correct—in theory. But let us examine now the practice of it in China.

I had one of the biggest surprises of my life when it was announced at a monster rally in the Peking Workers' Stadium that the leader of the Nationalist Party's Revolutionary Committee (Kuomintang) was going to speak. The occasion was a mass meeting to reaffirm support for the Bandung principles. Some of the delegates at the anniversary celebrations of the original Bandung conference had come from Indonesia to attend the meeting at Peking, including Mr Abdullahi Diallo of Guinea. I don't remember the details of what the Nationalist Party leader said, but his address didn't differ from what I had been accustomed to hear from any secretary of the Chinese Communist Party.

There is only one party that matters in China: the

Communist Party. The Nationalists and other minority parties, however, are permitted to maintain a skeleton organisation to keep their name on record. There are about eight such 'dummy' parties. Their leaders may hold government posts, but all they do and say is dictated by the Communist Party. This is really no more than a stratagem to deceive the world into thinking that China has a multi-party, democratic system. One of the official guides during my tour of North Korea put it very neatly when, in answer to my queries, he explained that, though North Korea has several parties, all the others had to operate under the aegis of the Workers' Party, which is the local version of the Communist Party.

It appears to me that, by this make-believe of a multi-party system, the Communist Party admits the need for an outward semblance of democracy as the term is understood elsewhere. It has deliberately suppressed all genuine representation of other political viewpoints, but it finds it advantageous to keep their shadows in being.

In a government which is truly *by* the people, any organ which controls the people's destiny—parliament, assembly and so forth—must be elected by the people themselves, not appointed or imposed by any one party. In a country of several different parties, where independents also have the right, not only in theory, but in practice as well, to stand for election, the people can be said to be fairly well represented by candidates of the various political parties and by independents. But where only a single party exists to put up candidates, the question arises as to how fairly the people are represented, particularly when, as in the case of China, the wishes of the Party are not identifiable in many matters with the wishes of the people.

I witnessed an example of democratic election, Chinese

style, at the Medical College in Peking in the spring of 1962. The new term had just begun and it was necessary to elect officers to fill five vacant posts in our class. The Party's agent in the class wrote down the names of five candidates on the board, after which ballot papers were distributed. All the five candidates were 'elected'. I have never witnessed a national election in China, but I'm convinced those students were doing what their elders do at election time. Were these five students really elected, or were they just appointed by the Party? Are 'people's deputies' really elected, or are they appointed by the Party? For an election to be worthy of the name, the voters need to be given the opportunity of a genuine choice. There can be no such genuine choice when nominations come from one source only. I became convinced that it is only the Communist Party's 'approved candidates' who get into the national assembly. But the Chinese call this democracy.

When Lincoln said 'for the people', I understand him to have meant 'for the benefit of the people'. What do we find in China? The people grow lean with hunger while those appointed to govern for their benefit grow fat. Given a free choice, I think it is highly likely that the Chinese would prefer more tractors for the fields than tanks for the army, more chemical fertilisers for the soil than explosives for bombs. What is certain is that they have not been given an opportunity to express their choice. As matters stand, it is always the Party that chooses for them, claiming that it does so in their name and 'for them'. 'Theirs not to reason why, theirs but to do and die!'

But the communist method does not limit itself to 'fixing' elections so as to achieve the upper hand. Through propaganda and political indoctrination, as well as through direct acts, it tries to condition the minds of the people to accept as good and proper what the Party holds to be good and proper. The Chinese communist will tell you that human rights and those freedoms of expression and of religion which true democrats hold dear are fully maintained in China. But the fact is that, whatever some clause in the constitution may say about fundamental rights, the people are under such constant pressure to express the Party's 'correct' line that, for fear of saying the wrong thing the average Chinese in public will keep his mouth tightly shut or else say the most commonplace things, or simply bore you to death by repeating a 'correct' statement of the Party's line. I had two 'friends' in the Institute of Modern Languages, one in the English department and the other studying Spanish. When they went home on summer vacation, each wrote me a letter telling me how happy all the commune peasants were and how everyone was expecting a bumper harvest. The one letter could easily have been a copy of the other. They were telling me what the Party decreed should be told. There was none of those private remarks and intimate details that make a friend's letter a pleasure to read.

A good example of how a 'freedom' is handled in China is provided by the régime's religious policy. The Party has effectively combined two methods for dealing with religion: outright persecution, and the substitution of the communist ideology for all other beliefs. Before the Party came to power, the Chinese people were ardent worshippers. Taoism, Christianity, Islam, Buddhism and I know not how many more religions flourished side by side. But today the Party preaches there are neither gods nor God, only communism, and they have taken steps to ensure the elimination of religion. The Party argues that the Christian missionaries were expelled because they were imperialists or imperialist agents. It is easy for us colonial and ex-colonial people, who are familiar with the 'bible in one hand, sword in the other' tactics of Western imperialism, to sympathise a good deal with this argument. But what of the Chinese Brahmins and Moslems? Were they all imperialists and imperialist agents too?

The problems arising from an expatriate clergy are not confined to China. The problem exists in Africa and it is not an easy one to solve. In many cases, expatriate clergy are an embarrassment both to their religion and to the state they live under. But equally the work they do is in many cases absolutely vital for the religious communities they serve, work that is wanted and respected by large sections of the people. In some instances expatriate church leaders, not being so vulnerable as native-born clergymen to the indirect or direct pressures of the state authorities, can more freely express the standpoint of their congregations on controversial questions. Often this leads to uneasy relations between the church and the new state, as we saw in the case of President Nkrumah's expulsion of the Anglican Bishop of Accra. Some in Africa want to wage an ideological struggle against the religions that embrace all races and communities, either to foster a racialist nationalism or else substitute a new state religion or personality cult, or both. Anything that can weaken the international and interracial character of these religions is seized on. But the African is deeply religious; he has accepted Christianity or Islam as the case may be as his own in the place of paganism. It is not going to be easy to dislodge Africans from their religious loyalties. As President Nkrumah was finally made to realise, there is something called public opinion which no leader can afford to ignore absolutely in countries whose people have not yet submitted themselves to slavery under an all-powerful party or state.

This is the main difference in the matter of religion between Africa and China. The Chinese religious communities could not stand up against the communist régime, not simply because they were 'tainted' by identification with foreigners, but also because the people were conditioned, by promises, by hope for better things, and by fear, into accepting the Party's will as paramount in all things.

In Peking and other cities in China, I saw the Christian churches still standing with their crosses atop of them. So there really is religious freedom in China? Before you think so, you must realise that the majority of the churches have been turned to more 'realistic' uses, as stores and warehouses. The crosses remain because they are valuable for communist propaganda. As the foreign delegate is sped through the streets, his guide points out the cross and says: 'There is one of our churches'; and ten to one the visitor will go home to praise China's freedom of worship.

In Hanchow, I saw magnificent Buddhist temples, some with statues as high as a two-storey building. Those temples are now museum-pieces. The Buddhist priests have all of a sudden 'discovered' that their religion is nonsense and have given up their temples to the state.

Peking has a Christian church and a Moslem mosque that are still tolerated. It is here where foreigners, diplomatists and visitors worship. A foreign friend of mine went to church on Easter Day 1961. There was a devout congregation present, but only one lone Chinese. Peking with its six million people used to have many thousands of Christians. Now only one will attend worship on Easter Day. Very well; a good many of them may have been 'rice Christians', and now the Christian rice has gone, their faith has gone with it. But there were also very many sincere believers. Why don't they come to church? Doesn't the Party maintain that there is perfect freedom of worship in China? Why don't they exercise that freedom? The fact is, as with all the other freedoms and rights which the Party says are maintained in China, the people don't exercise the right of free worship because they dare not.

I know of countries where the government and the accredited representatives of the people, having in full parliament put forward laws and decisions, have been forced to repeal those laws or modify those decisions, notwithstanding their legality, because the people have made it clear in no uncertain terms that they will not put up with them. Full democracy is where the people have at their disposal all the instruments necessary to make their opinions felt in the highest quarters: the press, radio, free discussions and, where necessary, public demonstrations and strikes.

But in 'democratic' China, these instruments either do not exist or they are under the absolute control of the Party. Even free discussion between private individuals has become a risky business because of the prevalence of spies and informers. No one ever demonstrates in China, except in favour of the Party and on instruction from the Party. No one ever even mentions the word 'strike', much less sets about organising one.

The Chinese Communist Party and all other communist parties pay democracy the compliment vice gives to virtue—hypocrisy. They realise that democracy to millions and millions the world over is a desirable ideal. And so they deem it worthwhile to keep up a democratic façade in their régimes, and by deceptions and fraud to give the outside world the impression that their régimes are democratic. The façades are sometimes so elaborate that even intelligent people are deceived. It took me many months and thousands of miles of travel in China, North Korea and Russia to discover how artificial that façade is, how thin the veneer of democracy. It is not surprising that many Africans, so far away from the reality, should fail to see what a hollow thing communist 'democracy' is.

Democracy, I believe, presupposes freedom of speech and of movement, of the press, of religion; freedom from fear, freedom to choose and practise the vocation of one's choice; and respect for the law of the land and other men's rights within a system which admits of constitutional changes. Where these fundamental human rights and freedoms are deliberately suppressed, there is not democracy.

In China I saw only a *government of the people, by the Party for the Party*. A far cry from the ideal of democracy.

PART II

African Students in China

9

Comings and Goings

All students arriving in China are first admitted into the
Institute of Foreign Languages, Peking, where they have
to study the Chinese language before entering the
universities. With another student of your own nationality, you share a little room of about 8 ft by 10 ft. The
room has two small beds, two wardrobes, two study
tables and two chairs. On your first day in the school
you are supplied with a blanket, a quilt for winter use,
two bed-spreads, one pillow together with its cover, a
cake of soap and a wash-basin. You have to make these
articles last you the six or seven years of your stay in
China. The room you occupy is rent-free and every
month you receive a subsistence allowance of 100 yuan
(about £15). With this allowance you buy food, drink and
smokes, clothes and every other article or service that
will require money. During the autumn term of the
1960–61 academic year, the allowance for all foreign
students was 80 yuan (about £12) a month. But during
the winter vacation, students (mainly African) began to
grumble so loudly that the Chinese were forced to increase the allowance to 100 yuan monthly. To the
Chinese we must have looked a really ungrateful lot for
demanding a rise, considering that Chinese students
were receiving a meagre 10 yuan (about thirty shillings)
monthly and graduate teachers 40 yuan (about £6)
monthly. But the fact is that we simply could not live on

the starvation ration offered to Chinese students and tutors and were therefore spending approximately five times the amount a normal Chinese spent on food per month. Towards the end of 1961 and beginning of 1962 the food shortage had become so bad that each foreign student was eating ten times as much food as his Chinese counterpart, not so much in quantity as in quality.

Attached to the mess-hall is a buffet where foreign students alone may buy biscuits, candies, fruits, drinks (both soft and alcoholic) and cigarettes; these articles are not easily obtainable in the city. There is also a small hardware shop where they may buy articles of clothing and toilet.

At the beginning of 1961, the Chinese embarked upon a project which was intended to provide foreign students with accommodation more suitable for them than the gloomy houses they were occupying, while at the same time giving them a practical demonstration of the Great Leap Forward. Three buildings were meant to be ready for occupation by the opening of the 1961–2 academic year, that is, by September 1, 1961. But like everything else that is built in the New China, they were supposed to be finished ahead of schedule—that's part and parcel of the Great Leap Forward. The builders actually made a brave effort in the forward-leaping but it seems something went very wrong with the mechanism of their leaping muscles. The buildings were still unfinished more than six months after the date fixed for their completion.

*   *   *

Of the African nationalities that were in China at my time, all except one (Chad Republic) were sponsored either by their home governments or by political parties and organisations at home, and all were on scholarships offered by the Chinese government through its sub-sidiary organs—the All-China Federation of Labour, the All-China Federation of Women, the Afro-Asian Solid-arity Committee and the Sino-African Friendship Associa-tion. A fairly large proportion of us had already absorbed a good deal of socialism from our political parties, though I am not positive we were all sure what the whole socialism business was about.

Before we arrived in China our ignorance about the country was almost perfect. Some knew nothing at all about it beyond what the geography books say, and the majority were under the false impression, communicated by Chinese propagandists and visiting African delegates, that China was a veritable paradise on earth. The jolt such students received was ruder by far than that to those whose minds on China were almost a blank to begin with.

The chart overleaf shows the African nationalities that were in China, their original numerical strength, the students that have since quit China because they were dissatisfied with conditions, the number now left in that country and, finally, the number that was also threatening to quit by the time I left in April 1962.

Though the Zanzibari students had demanded re-patriation some days earlier than I did, I left before them because the General Secretary of their home party had cabled them instructions to hold on till he himself went over to China to see what he could do about their griev-ances. He could do nothing about them apparently. They are all back in Africa now.

With only a few exceptions, the Camerounian students also hankered after repatriation, but they had some special problems in addition to what every student who decided to go home had to face. They belonged to the

Roll of African Student Nationalities in China
1961–2

Country	Came to China	Left China for Home	Still in China	Threatening to leave
Chad Republic	1	Nil	1	Nil
Congo (Gizenga government)	3	3	Nil	Nil
Ghana	4	3	1	Nil
Cameroun (UPC)	36	34	2	Nil
Kenya	2	2	Nil	Nil
Somalia	48	30	18	10
S. Rhodesia	1	1	Nil	Nil
Sudan	1	1	Nil	Nil
Uganda	4	4	Nil	Nil
Zanzibar	18	18	Nil	Nil
UAR	Figures not well known			
Total	118	96	22	10

Except in the case of Cameroun and Zanzibar, all figures are given as up to April 1962.

Union des Populations du Cameroun (UPC), a party still seriously at loggerheads with their home government. According to them, their government had promulgated a law depriving of citizenship anyone who travelled to the socialist countries. (A Camerounian diplomatist later denied the existence of such a law. Any law-abiding citizen, he said, was welcome in the Cameroun republic.) If there was such a law, then they were technically no longer Camerounian. For them repatriation could only mean smuggling themselves into the country and im-

mediately joining the rebels in the maquis, or else loiter-
ing in some other foreign land. For these reasons they
were less reckless than the other nationalities in talking
about repatriation.

In September 1962, however, thirty out of the thirty-
two Camerounian students left in China at the time I
departed were expelled, at least so went the press an-
nouncement. (Of the original thirty-six Camerounians
one, a girl, had already left to join her fiancé in Moscow,
another went home for health reasons, and two more left
on instructions from the Vice-President of their party.)
Despite many efforts I have not yet been able to discover their present whereabouts and the reason for their
expulsion. As to the latter I can make an intelligent guess.

The Camerounians, who had organised themselves
into a disciplined branch of their party in China, declared a
dispute with the Chinese when the latter refused to repatriate one of their number by name Nyobe. This man
Nyobe, they said, was acting in collusion with the
Chinese and against the interest of their party and their
revolution. He was consequently expelled from the UPC.
Since Nyobe held his scholarship solely by virtue of party
membership, they argued, his expulsion from the party
should automatically annul his scholarship. The Chinese
were accepting none of it, however. After a long tug, the
Camerounians had to set a date for a protest hunger
strike which, after much pleading by the comrades, they
decided to withold. An incident involving another
Chinese collaborator, Muzong (Camerounian), of whom
you will be reading more in Chapter 14, may possibly
have complicated matters.

Before I left China there was not much doubt in my
mind about the possibility of such mass expulsions. The
Chinese had brought us to their country for a definite
purpose: to absorb their indoctrination. But far from

taking kindly to it, we laughed at it. It is logical to expect that they would seek fresh and more absorbent
material elsewhere. Also, talks I had with comrade Chen
Yu (member of the People's Congress and Head of the
International Department of the Labour Federation)
made me think they could not long continue to support
any sizeable foreign student population. Funds were
running low, the comrade lamented. What was more,
foreigners needed special food, very difficult to obtain in
today's China.

Though the Congo broke off diplomatic relations with
Red China, the Congolese students could have stayed
behind if they had wanted to. The Education Minister
himself found it necessary to stoop so low as to plead
with them to remain, but they were already fed up with
China. They packed their bags and left.

10

Background to the Exodus

The causes of the student exodus, which began around the middle of 1961, are as follows:

1 *Undesirable political indoctrination*
Just a few weeks in China made it plain that the real purpose in inviting us to their country was not to educate us to help build our respective countries, but rather to indoctrinate us with Marxist politics. The very nature of our language lessons led to that conclusion. From the very beginning we were taught, almost exclusively, political vocabulary, so that within a few months we could listen to and understand complicated political discussions; but when it came to every-day conversation we fell flat—we didn't have the vocabulary.

To illustrate my point here are twelve sentences translated from the first three textbooks for beginners:

1. The whole world will certainly develop in the direction of communism; this is a law of social evolution.
2. The people's communes, like a newly risen sun, light the path of progress for the Chinese people.
3. Communist society is the most ideal society.
4. No matter what work we do, we must depend upon the Party's leadership.
5. One can never speak enough of the Party's goodness.

6 Imperialists and all reactionaries are paper tigers.

7 I shall never forget what the Party has taught me.

8 Before liberation the peasants suffered under the oppression and exploitation of the landlords; they toiled from dawn to dusk, but still could have neither enough food nor warm clothes.

9 We shall certainly do the work according to the Party's direction.

10 Humanity's most ideal society—the communist society—will certainly prevail everywhere in the world.

11 The October socialist revolution opened a new era in the history of mankind; from that time began the new world revolution led by the proletariat.

12 The Party calls upon all youth to study Chairman Mao's works and to become good students of Chairman Mao.

This treatment of their language—introducing politics to the almost total exclusion of everything else—so discouraged me that after a really enthusiastic and successful beginning, I contented myself with just doing the bare minimum to get the hang of the language. After six months of instruction, I found myself begging one of our tutors to tell me how to say 'water' in Chinese. 'Water' isn't politics, and so we hadn't been taught it. Using a Chinese dictionary is a bit of a detective feat, and English–Chinese dictionaries were not available to us then. Under pressure from us foreign students the authorities finally introduced newly-prepared textbooks with less politics, but those were still unsatisfactory. It was due also to pressure from us that they introduced a course in science vocabulary—a course which, I must say frankly, helped a great deal in removing the difficulties we would have encountered had we entered our faculties after feeding exclusively on political vocabulary.

As if the politics in our textbooks were not enough, our teachers introduced a 'history' course. The 'history' was just more politics. After a few lessons of this many of us refused to attend any more; we were not there for politics, we argued.

One Saturday morning our tutors organised a forum to discuss the 'history' we had studied so far. The first topic for discussion was: 'Why do the Chinese people sympathise with the liberation struggles of the oppressed peoples of the world?' When this topic had been dealt with by our tutors, I was absent from the class, but I had my own ideas. A little devil possessed me that morning and I opened the discussion.

The Chinese people sympathise with the oppressed peoples of the world, I said, because their own sufferings under the imperialists and colonialists are so recent in their memory that they are able to understand precisely how the oppressed people feel. The British, French and American people, I went on, suffered from foreign domination once, but their experiences are so remote in their past that they cannot easily appreciate what it is like to be oppressed.

The first part of my answer the Chinese hailed with joy. But then I continued to my second point. The Chinese people sympathise with the oppressed peoples because they want to win markets. I explained: the colonial and ex-colonial peoples know the colonialists for their exploitation and, for this reason, we may want to break loose our Western economic bonds and seek new horizons as soon as we gain our freedom. Seeking new horizons, where else could we turn but to those very people who, during our liberation struggles, showed us sympathy? The underdeveloped countries close to China do not constitute a sufficiently wide market. China must expand her markets, particularly to Africa.

This part of my answer was received in stolid silence. Nothing loath, I went on to point three. The Chinese people want to spread communism to the newly liberated areas of the world. Since the now oppressed peoples have always heard that communism means something like transfer to paradise and since under the capitalist colonialists they have only known merciless exploitation and oppression comparable to hell, it is not impossible that, when the colonial people finally throw off their shackles, they will want to experiment with a novel system which presents itself as diametrically opposed to capitalism.

This last part of my answer also had no enthusiastic reception. When I had said my say the Chinese protested vehemently against my reactionary and heretical ideas. No, they didn't want markets. No, they were not anxious to propagate communism. Of the eight other African students present at the forum only one supported me. But then, exactly one week after my heresy, the Chinese government signed a trade agreement with Nigeria. China now has trade agreements with several other African countries. I do not mean to say that trade agreements with Red China are bad, provided they are of mutual benefit to both parties. But why deny that they want markets? What is the purpose of their trade exhibitions and missions in Africa if not to capture and expand markets?

About the communists' desire to make their ideology penetrate every nook and cranny of the earth, I need make no further comment. It is already too well known all over the world that that is their intention.

Citing this history lesson incident may seem a little out of place here, but I do it to stress a specific point which will enable my readers to understand many of the apparently odd things that we students did. I happened to have been completely without prejudice, either for or against China, before I went to that country. Because of this very neutrality of attitude I found myself one of the first to develop hostility towards the Chinese system. Many of the others bravely kept up their original pro-socialist appearances till they became so fed up with the show that they swung violently against China. And what a mighty swing that was! I virtually found myself (as Secretary-General of our Students' Union) standing at the pivotal point of a Black versus Yellow tug, alternately pacifying or rebuking this or the other side.

What I seek to illustrate is that Black-Yellow mutual hostility (the comrades, I may say, kept up the anaemic pretence of friendship much better than we did) and the utter frustration of us students so developed in bitterness that we threw all pretence and caution to the winds and spoke exactly as we thought. Speaking as one thinks is what you would normally expect from any free and normal human being (except diplomatists and politicians who are not really normal while on duty), but this happens to be an offence in China. You are expected to speak as the Party speaks. Thus, I was committing an unpardonable offence when, instead of launching into an eulogium of China's tender sympathies to the oppressed peoples of the world, I plunged into a heresy about trade markets and the world communist movement.

Of course, the original question was wrong in the first place. Wrong, because of the word *sympathise*; it should really have been *pretend to sympathise*. If the Chinese people really do sympathise with oppressed people, how can we explain their having gone out of their way to oppress Tibet? How can we explain their expansionist and imperialist activities against India? Sympathise, my foot!

As a result of too much politics in everything, some students refused to attend classes any further. They just lazed around until the authorities finally agreed to their request for repatriation.

2 *Language difficulty*

There were some students who plainly could not cope with the language. There is no plain-sailing in the study of Chinese. Though the grammar is remarkably simple, there are the Chinese characters to cope with. I have already explained in Chapter 2 some of the difficulties involved.

The language was an insurmountable barrier only to a few, however. The rest finished in eight months (excluding vacation periods) the course the Chinese had planned to take two years. We could really have taken much less time at the language, but because we grew disgusted with the politics with which the textbooks were packed full we went slow and spent much time agitating for changes or regularly tearing out the most unashamedly political texts. Besides, many students were most of the time wavering between staying on and clearing out altogether; they had little incentive for serious effort.

3 *Poor educational standards*

In Chinese education, the most prominent subject overall is politics. Four or five mortal hours of politics each week amount to between sixteen and twenty hours per month or from 144 to 180 hours in a nine-month academic year. Add to this the time occupied by innumerable political meetings each week, and you will have an idea of the amount of time wasted in Chinese universities on politics which is entirely unconnected with one's branch of study. In the Language Institute where foreigners attend classes all by themselves, their summer vacation starts long in advance of that of the Chinese, because foreigners do no manual labour. In institutions where foreigners attend classes together with Chinese, the foreigners have extra vacations during the period the comrades are off to the farms, with the result that, excluding national holidays, foreign students have about a hundred days of holiday per annum as against about sixty for Chinese. In some institutions, of which the Peking Medical College is an example, courses have recently been extended by a full year. They had discovered that without this extension the students had to skip many parts of their course scheme in order to pass out within the original period of five years.

As I have already demonstrated (Chapter 2), the medical course in the China I know leaves much to be desired. It is entirely wrong to judge Chinese doctors by the brilliant performances of a few of their number, such as in the case of the burnt steel worker. Many of the old hands, trained in Japan, the United States, France and other countries may be as good as doctors anywhere else in the world. The new crop of communist doctors, however, appears to be wanting in much. The incompetence of Chinese doctors was always a regular topic of discussion among foreign students. Most of us had had our individual experiences and no one ever appeared impressed by their performance. I knew a foreign student, a girl, who was so seriously ill that we all feared for her, but who obstinately refused to go to hospital. Because drugs were in rather short supply doctors gave the patient '*a-si-pi-li-ni*', alias aspirin, for almost every ailment. That girl did not care for more aspirin. Even if that was psychotherapy instead of chemotherapy, it looked a little like over-doing it. Another girl who had lain in a solitary bed in the Third Medical Hospital (attached to my college) for several weeks, simply walked out on her doctors and into the full blast of Peking winter—in her pyjamas. Rather a silly thing to do, but I am not sure I wouldn't have done the same under the circumstances.

It sounds incredible, but it is nevertheless true, that Chinese graduates of the Foreign Language Institute do make monstrous grammatical mistakes like, 'the boys is . . . ' And don't take it for a slip of tongue; they just don't know that they have made a mistake and will repeat it another time. We found it difficult to believe that those people had been trained in their respective foreign languages for five whole years. The Chinese authorities, however, must have thought very highly of those graduates, seeing that they were appointed to teach in a college. Could such scholastic standards have given us foreigners any confidence in Chinese institutions of learning?

4 *Social life*

Throughout our life in China there was one constant headache: How to combine work and play in such acceptable proportions as to avoid being dull Jacks and Jills. Of work there was of course enough and to spare, but of normal diversion and entertainment, there was always sore dearth. I have already mentioned that Peking has only one night club, the International Club, reserved for foreign diplomatists and delegates. We foreign students used to smuggle ourselves in at times when we grew desperate. Well dressed people were extremely rare sights in China, and if you did see any, ten to one they were foreigners, probably diplomatists. So what some students usually did when they wanted to enjoy a Saturday evening at the International was to dress in their smartest suit—bow tie, shiny black shoes and all —and just walk in as boldly as if the place belonged to them. The stewards usually accepted them without much ado. It was as simple as all that: just *look like* a

diplomat and you were through. If someone had accused
us of 'impersonation', we would promptly have pleaded
'extenuating circumstances'. We had arguments in
abundance to substantiate the plea.

Dance parties were held on the campuses, but these
were rather peculiar affairs. In the beginning, music
used to be provided by a Chinese student band. But it
made no attempt whatever at real dance music. Chinese
bands have three standard songs (one of them is *Socialism
is good*) they play over and over again till you are ready
to burst your spleen in sheer exasperation and boredom.
In a year I never heard anything like a new hit. They
presumably could not afford to take much time off from
politics to learn anything new in music apart from the
very poor Soviet imitations they had learnt years ago.
But what really knocked all interest out of their dances
for us was that, whereas there was no trouble when a
Chinese boy danced with a Chinese girl, things began to
grow rather awkward when an African boy danced with
a Chinese girl. Immediately you left the girl, some tutor
or Youth League activist was sure to go running to her
to scrutinise her about the subject of your conversation
during the dance. The girl was in duty bound as a good
socialist to confess as requested or else suffer the penalty of
being 'criticised'. (And 'criticised' in Chinese communist
jargon can mean anything from mild rebuke to outright
condemnation to hard labour in the communes.)

To overcome all the difficulties entailed in going to
Chinese dances, some students amongst us badgered the
authorities into buying a saxophone and a trumpet for
the exclusive use of foreign students. It was a real
delight when our three-piece band (add a guitar) got
going. In our attempt to create a social atmosphere more
to our tastes, we made every slight excuse the occasion
for a regular gaudeamus. National independence

anniversaries, anniversaries of the foundation of home parties or of the assassination of our heroes and, on one occasion, the umpteenth commemoration of the death of somebody's mother—these were all celebrated with speeches, dances and drinking sessions, as the solemnity or frivolity of the occasion demanded. As a result we were promptly accused of having 'bourgeois capitalistic tastes'. But if I must be frank I would rather have bourgeois capitalistic tastes than no taste at all!

Film shows were an important item of entertainment (?) during the earlier part of our sojourn. The films were usually either about their revolution or about the Korean war. The revolutionary films have an exasperating habit of ending on the same theme: while a gallant revolutionary hero lies wounded and dying, surrounded by anxious comrades, a young zealot comes running across the screen waving a voluminous red flag signifying the victory of the revolution. In China I never once saw a science fiction film or any film that stirred your imagination or at least showed that the producers knew what imagination means. When a man has had politics all day long, in his lessons, in private conversation and in almost every other activity, it is just asking too much to expect that he will be entertained by supposed entertainment that is purely political in background and/or content. Films on the Korean war usually depict a handful of Chinese volunteers showing such outsize gallantry that for them it is no problem to hold at bay and finally to route an entire tank-supported infantry battalion of United Nations troops. I have no doubt that a handful of fanatics can actually work wonders on the battlefield, but after seeing the Chinese volunteers in action a couple of times, I decided they were so awfully brave that I did not care to see them in action again. Voluminous red banners also lost all their interest in a few weeks. The other African students did not think better of these films either. There were times when film shows planned exclusively for us had to be cancelled because there was no attendance. It often took many tutors and interpreters canvassing from room to room to get a handful of students to attend a showing. And yet it was free! All things considered, those tutors really tried to please us, but they failed miserably due to no fault of their own. The fault lay entirely in the attitude of the Chinese Communist Party, who would reshape everything, down even to public entertainment, to serve its political ends.

Peking has a number of very impressive public parks where one could take a walk or go boating or swimming. Almost without exception the Party inherited these parks from the emperors and mandarins. The four most notable are the Summer Palace Park, the North Sea Park, the Coal Hill Park and the Forbidden City or Winter Palace. A walk in the parks is the form of entertainment most easily accessible to, and most widely patronised by, the citizenry. We also tried it and enjoyed it, but there remained some inconveniences. The parks were far away and the only food or snacks available there were rationed as well as being so costly we could not easily afford them. (In the North Sea Park I once bought four biscuits for 4 yuan, about thirteen shillings; in West Africa those biscuits would together have cost a shilling at most.) If we forced ourselves to go to the parks, it was for purposes quite different from relaxation. I shall mention these presently.

There was another kind of 'entertainment' we tried but with no marked success. This consisted in just making friends. We made or wanted to make friends, first, because successful friendly relations would help us to know China, and secondly, for all the other reasons that

E

can lead a normal human being to want friends. We had two distinct types of friends in China. In the one category were those foisted upon us by the school authorities, and in the other were those we made ourselves. During our early days many Chinese students, mainly boys, approached us with intent to make friends. We accepted them readily because we were anxious to get acquainted. Through no fault of our own, we foreigners formed a segregated colony in the school, eating, studying, sleeping separately and even having separate entertainment, with the result that, though living in the capital of China, we knew extremely little about what the Chinese were really like. But as time went on we gradually learnt that these 'friends' were not really friends at all but rather people set upon us by the authorities to report on almost everything we did. They reported on the books we read, the people we met, the usual topics of our conversation and on every other matter that could help the authorities to determine whether our level of socialist consciousness was rising, falling or simply static. (The more books of Marx, Engels, Lenin and Mao you had on your bookshelf the higher you were in the estimation of the Chinese.) We grew very resentful when we made the discovery about the informers, particularly as students who had no specific instructions to spy on us were strictly warned against associating with us. We had a 'bourgeois capitalist mentality', the authorities told them; any association with us might lead to a degeneration of their socialist consciousness.

I don't know what guest, however polite, can suffer such insult from his host without reaction. We, on our part, did react. We reacted by making friends of our own choice, much to the annoyance of the Chinese. When we chose our own friends, we did not care much about the Chinese boys any more; we made a bee-line for the girls.

This was a natural form of association for any normal male. The fact that friendship between African boy and Chinese girl was taboo did not discourage us a bit; it rather spurred us on. We went ahead making the Chinese know we were fully aware of the attempt to discriminate against us even in matters of friendship, but that we were bent on choosing our own friends. This brought about much friction and bitterness on both sides. The African students, on the one hand, were bitterly resentful of calculated attempts to make their lives unbearable; the Chinese, on the other hand, were fearful of our uncontrolled association with other Chinese citizens who had not yet received instructions on how to behave towards us. Keeping us to ourselves as much as possible was a necessary precaution through which the Chinese intended us to know only what came from the Party and its mouth-pieces. We wrecked that plan by being too wilful, and learnt many things as a punishment.

Sino-African relations were in no way improved by the fact that such girl friends as we were able to make were packed off to prison or to the commune farms for hard labour almost as fast as we made them, their only crime being that they dared to make friends with Africans, contrary to the Party's orders. When piteous letters began to pour in from victimised girls and their relatives telling what had happened and why, and asking their friends to keep up hope, we promptly changed our tactics. Girl friends did not visit us on the campus any more. To dodge the security men always posted at our gates, some simply watching and others officially noting name of visitor, business, entry time, exit time, when, where and how acquainted, etc., the public parks became the usual rendezvous. But then, secret service men abound everywhere and a black or brown African countenance could never be effectively hidden in a

crowd of yellow faces. It was enough for a girl to be
seen walking with an African for her doom to be sealed.

Where they could not bind or punish us directly
without raising an unholy rumpus, they achieved the
same end by punishing those close to us. Men whom
threats and bodily torture could never break are known
to have been broken by the sight or the prospect of
people dear to them suffering molestation for their sake.
The Chinese authorities knew their business just too
well.

5 *Hostility*

Among our woes 'manufactured' directly or indirectly
by the Party, was the people's hostility towards us. The
Chinese must have been a good-natured people, but
modelled to the Party's blue-print they became veritable
dragons. Who would blame a Chinese worker for being
hostile to African students when he, who toils to contri-
bute to their scholarship funds, is left half-starving on
evil-smelling cabbage while the foreigners can eat good
food in almost unlimited quantities? Or when he is made
to drink and smoke the worst concoctions and clothe
himself in the poorest garments while the foreigners imported by the Party can have the best in the land? And
how could Chinese students be expected to put up easily
with the fact of being packed eight to a room with a
monthly allowance of 10 yuan while foreigners in the
same institution lived one or two in a room and had 100
yuan each per month? Could Chinese tutors put up kindly
with the idea of being paid 40 yuan monthly, not even
half as much as their foreign students took? And what of
the dean of an institution who has to receive the same
pay as his foreign students?

If you had been waiting in a bus queue in the cold,
cold winter for half an hour, and then seen someone

stalking right to the head of the queue as if he were boss
of the whole place, what would have been your reaction?
Yet we foreign students were specifically instructed to
jump queues, to ignore the feelings of those very people
whose toil bought the buses. I must indulge in a little
self-praise. We did not use to jump queues. We used to
compete and struggle, like the common people. In China
nobody stands to yield seats to ladies. There are no ladies:
there are only comrades. But people always yield seats to
nursing mothers—and foreigners. As the foreign student
enters a bus or train, the conductor *orders* the nearest
Chinese to stand and give up his or her seat. The people
used to stand—with very evident bad grace—but they
used to stand all right: Party's Orders.

Were such people being helped to love the foreigners?

In my country I would willingly and voluntarily give
priority to the foreigner in order to demonstrate my
country's brand of hospitality. But to stand because a
party commands it is a frightfully tall order. That tall
order Chinese nationals were expected to obey—without
question.

All these things did actually happen. Foreign students
were many times better off than the Chinese students,
workers and peasants. We foreigners never did a thing to
merit this privileged treatment. Our only claim to it, a
claim which, by the way, we never made ourselves, was
that we were supposed to be good material to absorb
communist indoctrination and afterwards spill it back to
the people in our native countries.

It is to be expected that the Party itself, after granting
us all those privileges to impress us and make us swallow
their ideology with as little mental agony as possible,
should in its turn grow hostile when it discovered that,
rather than accept their ideology without question, we
spared no effort to bring it into ridicule. The Party did

grow hostile and we did not fail to notice it even though party and school officials continued to wear the same old hypocritical smiles.

Speaking for myself, I have to say that at no time did my home organisation (the Ghana Trades Union Congress) or home government make me understand that the main aim of sending me to China was to make a good Marxist of me. I am unable to say whether that was their intention, nor do I know whether there was any mutual discussion or agreement between my home organisation or government and the Chinese. But I maintain that anyone wanting me to change my old beliefs for other (even granting them better) beliefs must first convince me that the new beliefs are really superior to my old. And again, when I expected to be going to China to learn a profession and arrived only to find my hosts having something else in their minds even more important to them than the profession I had gone to study, I had every right to reconsider my position. My consent was never sought before they tried to ram their ideology down my throat. They had held out the offer of professional training as an attractive bait behind which they hid their sinister motives. I should have been asked back home whether or not I was prepared to help bring communist stuff into Africa. I should never have set foot in China had this been the condition. The communists had no right to be resentful of my rejection of their ideology. I never made them any promise of acceptance.

6 *Racial discrimination*

The Chinese have so long posed as defenders of the African and the persecuted races that it must really come as a shock to many people to hear that racial discrimination is practised in China. Chinese racial discrimination is not of the kind that springs spontaneously from the people. It is a deliberate attempt by the Communist Party to assert and to make the African accept once and for all the idea of the superiority of Yellow over Black. But we made them understand in very unequivocal terms that we were not prepared to add the burden of Yellow superiority to that of White superiority under which we and our forebears before us have been groaning for more years than we cared to count.

I would raise my hat to the memory of Albert Einstein, Mahatma Ghandi or Washington Carver any day, because of their pre-eminent contribution in their respective fields of endeavour, to the promotion of human knowledge and welfare. I would also, in courtesy, raise my hat to any African, Chinese, Eskimo or Malaysian for his or her worth as a man or woman. But the moment my action is prompted by the sole aim of gaining a favour, it drops from the elevated plane of courtesy to the mean one of ingratiation.

If Verwoerd were to propose a law granting to every African twice the normal pay of his white counterpart on the condition that Black and White still remain apart, many foolish Blacks might eagerly accept the condition. But, believe me, there would still be millions of idealistic Blacks who would make no compromise on racial segregation.

That is why it was that, while enjoying many benefits over and above those of our Chinese counterparts, we still raised our voices in loud condemnation of their racial discrimination. The Chinese lavished favours on us; but we understood all too clearly that they only sought to ingratiate themselves with us and thus make us more pliable for pro-communist moulding. We enjoyed the favours as such, but hated the motives. We wanted ourselves and, through us, our race, our people, to be accepted for our worth—just that. I shall have occasion to elaborate on the racial theme in another context.

7 *Spying*

Spying was by no means the least onerous of the many
burdens under which we had to labour in China. School
authorities have every right, nay the duty, to take
measures necessary for them to get acquainted with the
condition and general behaviour of their charges. But to
carry it so far that a student has almost no private life
of his own, that every private conversation or deed
becomes public through your Chinese 'friends', that the
foreign student should become the subject of character-
analysis in Chinese political classes, amounts to an abuse
of that right. If the Chinese had forgotten, we at least
did not forget, that every citizen has to exercise his
rights and freedoms with due respect to the rights and
freedoms of other citizens. If you have ever been spied
upon while you knew that your every movement was
under watch, you will perhaps understand how we were
always under constant mental tension and strain. The
Party thinks that to extract the maximum out of the
Chinese people it is necessary to keep them always on
edge. But then, we did not subscribe to that view, and we
would have none of it either.

*   *   *

For those who usually pooh-pooh stories brought back
from communist countries by African students, I re-
produce here an interesting article culled from the
pages of *West Africa*, September 1, 1962, page 959. It
speaks for itself.

> More than a week after the *Ghana Graphic*
> published photographs of students arriving at
> Accra Airport from Bulgaria with bandaged heads,
> two British newspapers have published circum-
> stantial stories of clashes in Sofia between African

and native students. This time the story does not seem to have been manufactured or exaggerated by publicity-hungry students—the students kept quiet. There should, however, be no surprise that such a clash has taken place—or that the local police have intervened violently on behalf of their own students. I believe that there was also a clash in Prague earlier this year. Though the occasion of the Sofia one is said to have been a Ghanaian's dancing with a Bulgarian girl, resentment against African students in these countries is due, visitors to them tell me, to the preferential treatment the governments offer the Africans, though the Africans themselves, used to much higher standards, are not satisfied and complain about segregation. Moreover the citizens of these countries are subjected to much propaganda before the recent arrival of African students in any number, suggesting that the Africans were poverty-stricken and had been deprived of education. But when they arrived, the African students were often much better clothed and owned possessions of much higher quality than the local people; often, too, they were more sophisticated than the local students who have come to resent preferential treatment for such visitors who appear, after all, not to need it. And since for so many years the citizens of communist countries have been so completely shielded from contact with people from non-communist countries, their theoretical devotion to world brotherhood has to contend with instinctive or induced xenophobia which in some cases might particularly affect Africans.

If I had been told that this man had written a précis of all that I have related about the life of African students in China, substituting only a few place names, I wouldn't have been surprised. But he hadn't. He writes of Bulgaria and I of China, and what we write has been further confirmed by the anti-African riots in Prague in the spring of 1963.

These, in short, are the reasons that led to the exodus. It was not confined to Africans either. There were Yemeni and Cuban students who also left because they were dissatisfied with conditions. The Chinese government and its agencies paid our fare to China. One would have thought that any student who was dissatisfied had just to tell the authorities 'I want to go home,' and then get his air or railway ticket with the minimum of delay. But the Chinese realised, as we also did, that every student returning home in disillusionment constituted an argument against China. Those students were not dumb; they could speak, and China's international reputation wasn't going to be improved if a whole lot of returned students started talking in the outside world in a big way. On one occasion, some Somali students who had gone back home circulated a pamphlet stating the conditions in China and giving reasons why they quit. Some time later a letter, purporting to come from the returned students, was sent in from Somalia condemning the pamphlet. The students all went back home for health reasons, the letter said. It was clear from the copy I read that either the students wrote that letter under duress from their party, or else someone else wrote it without their knowledge and consent. In either case, it must have been written at the instance of the Chinese. One of our Chinese tutors brought me my copy and triumphantly brandished it before my eyes. I asked him two simple questions. *First*, if the twenty-two Somalis left the paradise which is China only for health reasons, how is it the first batch found it necessary to stage a three-day hunger strike to be allowed to leave the paradise? *Secondly*, if all these students who had travelled thousands of miles to study for six or seven years were forced to leave China within less than a year because of ill health, then clearly this does not say much for the ability of Chinese doctors, does it?

The Chinese could find no answer to these questions; his face was redder than a Spanish tomato when he left me!

Therefore, the Chinese resisted any attempt by students to leave the country. Students were forced to adopt extreme measures to press their demand for repatriation. They went on hunger strikes. I was witness to one of these in spring 1961. (I cannot recall the exact date on which they started the strike, but I remember that it was just after our return from Shanghai where we had spent part of the winter vacation. That must have been in the month of March.) A group of five Somalis and one Sudanese had asked for repatriation because the Chinese had consistently refused to improve our conditions of living. They went in a body and plonked themselves down in armchairs in the President's reception room, refusing all food and refusing to leave till they were assured of their return tickets. The strike went on for about three days during which the Chinese piled the tables high with all sorts of delicacies they never thought of serving to us in quieter times. Mr Sokoro, head of the political party which sent the Somalis to China, was himself in the country at that time and had to ask the Chinese to repatriate any of his students who wanted it. It was only then that the comrades yielded and permitted the students to go home.

This hunger strike was actually the second in the series. There was one other in 1960 not long before I went to the country, involving twelve students from East and West Africa. They found conditions so horrible that they, one and all, demanded repatriation, but the

Chinese were having none of it. The students went on hunger strike. All of them, except one, Ibrahim of Sudan, finally went back home.

From those pioneers we learnt the value of hunger strikes and strikes in general as an instrument in our anti-Chinese struggles. These strikes were fully justifiable. There is never a concession a man can obtain from the Chinese by speaking soft. Softness and diplomacy are things those people do not seem to understand. The choice is between threatening them and getting what you want, or sitting tight and waiting till doomsday. We were not dealing with 'gentlemen'; we were dealing with 'comrades' who knew not what it was to be 'gentlemen'.

The Chinese lived in dread of demonstrations and strikes by foreign students. For one thing these served to show to the Chinese people that the Party is after all not as impregnable as it appears. Such activities could be a very bad moral example to Chinese nationals who, for their part, are never allowed to strike or demonstrate in any way except it be on the orders and to the benefit of the Party.

*   *   *

It would be absolutely wrong for anyone travelling in foreign parts to expect the host country to change its customs and ways to suit him. If any adaptation is needed it is the foreigner that must adapt himself to conditions in his host country and not *vice-versa*. One would have expected that our Chinese hosts, through suggestions and timely advice, would assist us to make necessary adjustments in our habits and ways. But no, by deliberate design, the Party saw to it that we were pampered with privileges we never asked for, and when we had learnt our lesson and would practise it, they grew

resentful. Very early during our stay in China I suggested to the Dean of Foreign Students in the Language
Institute that we foreigners be placed under the same
discipline as the Chinese students. I argued that to force
Chinese students to bed at 9 p.m. while allowing
foreigners to stay up to any hour they pleased, to grant
foreigners all sorts of extraordinary privileges and licence
that the Chinese could never enjoy, this could only
create friction between Chinese and foreigners, besides
lulling the foreigners into a false sense of immunity. On
another occasion, a Camerounian student named Jeppa
Hugo and I, acting for the African Students' Union,
went so far as to request that we Africans be permitted
to live together with the Chinese and mix freely with
them. We reasoned that, through living and mixing
with them, we would be compelled to converse in their
language and thus catch it faster. But then, that was
long before we got to know that the Chinese students
lived eight to a room. We had then been in the Institute
for about six months, but how could we have known the
condition of our fellow Chinese students when everything was done by the authorities to keep us apart?

Out of a total of 118 African students who studied in
China during my time, ninety-six have actually left and
a further ten had signified their intention to leave by
the time I packed by bags. This means that all together
approximately 90 per cent of the original number have
found something wrong with China—something which
made it impossible for them to stay longer.

African students are to be found studying in the
institutions of almost every advanced country in the
world. From what other country does 90 per cent of the
African student population return home in disgust within
a single academic year and without having completed
even half of what they were there to study?

Selected from the body of African youth, we were in no respect superior or inferior in brains or morals to the common run of African students in other foreign countries. And I must repel in advance any possible charge that we, or some sections of us, fell under the evil influence of those who, for some reason or other, did not want to continue in China. We were decidedly too individualistic a lot to allow the preparation of our several careers to be thus blasted by the influence of idlers. Why then, in contrast to other countries, should there be such a large percentage of drop-outs in China? Why should it happen that those among us who were pro-socialist of sorts before they ever stepped into China and who should, in the normal course of things, be most pro-Chinese (and were just that in the beginning), turned out in the long run to be the most vehemently anti-Chinese?

In my view it is because, firstly, China failed us miserably by not offering a standard and quality of education acceptable to us. Secondly, *we were disenchanted with socialism when we discovered that the Chinese brand of socialism was not the material of our dreams*—nor the nostrum by which we dreamed to cure all the ills of African society.

Africans have studied in foreign countries where, in the midst of plenty, they hungered and thirsted and suffered many other forms of privation. Some grew so desperate that they contemplated and even began the motions of suicide. But, somehow or other, they got through it all and, today, they are among the foremost and most respected leaders of Africa. To them it must have been a comfort that though the bush was thorny, the coveted rose was within arm's reach. They suffered, but they plucked the rose. But for us there was lacking the sustaining hope of reaching the final goal—sound education. We were suffering to no purpose. This purposelessness more than anything else made the majority of us back out.

No matter what the future holds I, for my part, will never regret my decision that Red China and I must go separate ways.

11

The African Students' Union

African students from Chad, Uganda, Cameroun and Kenya who had gone to China before me had tried to form a union in Peking University. They failed. Some said petty jealousies and intrigue among themselves wrecked their efforts. Others were sure their failure was due to Chinese interference. Notwithstanding that discouragement, we went ahead to make preparations for a new union. While preparatory discussions were going on, an incident occurred which, more than anything else, made us realise the need for such a union and spurred us on towards it. That incident was Lumumba's murder. We reasoned that, had we been more closely bound together, we would have had no difficulty in making our concerted voice heard on the issue. Disunited as we were, we could do no more than watch the Chinese making all the noise. Our decision was made. The union had to be formed at all costs.

The decision to start action was by no means even a quarter of the battle, however. In a country where all organisations including the so-called 'voluntary' ones are state initiated and run, getting official permission to form and run an independent union was rather a tricky business. We hit upon the idea of employing the same tricks as the communists are always playing on everybody. After having formed a preliminary 'ways and means committee' of seven members, we told the Chinese what we wanted. First, we wanted to hold an anti-imperialist demonstration and rally which would also be in protest against Lumumba's assassination; secondly, we wanted to form a union of all African students in China. The demonstration-cum-rally bait dangled in front of the Chinese noses worked wonders so far as the demonstration was concerned, but the Chinese were rather lukewarm towards the union. They insisted that we should go full speed ahead in preparations for the demonstration but that there was no hurry about permission to form our union. We, on our part, argued that any political activity by the African students must be within the framework of a representative union. We realised that following the Chinese advice would amount to our being used merely as instruments by the Chinese, particularly as they had expressed their readiness to foot the greater part of the bill. After several evenings of discussion, some lasting till the small hours of the morning, we decided it was high time we let fly a few hot words. We told the Chinese we were surprised that they who professed to support African unity should be reluctant to let Africans form a union in their country. In fact, we bluntly accused them of obstructing African unity. After we had generally made things rather unpleasant for the comrades, they yielded and gave us permission to go ahead with the union.

In the light of my later experiences in China, I can confidently say that the inability of the dean of Foreign students to give us an early decision was due to the fact that he had no power to do so. It is certain that the decision to permit the union's formation was taken somewhere within the unfathomable recesses of the Chinese Communist Party.

Preliminary preparations over, our union was launched

on March 18, 1961. Three *ad hoc* officers were elected to take charge of arrangements for the proposed rally and generally to supervise things till our constitution could be drafted and permanent officers elected.

Our three officers, Okidi of Uganda (President), John Hevi of Ghana (Secretary-General) and Abdallah of Chad (Finance Secretary), immediately set themselves to the task of preparing for the Africa Day celebrations due to be held in April. Our program was:

1 A cablegram to the Secretary-General of the United Nations expressing loss of confidence in his handling (or rather mishandling) of the Congo problem, asking him to quit his seat immediately and requesting that the United Nations wake up and take more realistic action in the Congo.

2 A cablegram to the All-African People's Conference, Accra, informing them of the formation of our union, supporting the Casablanca decision to form the African High Command and urging immediate action on implementing the decision (we were hoping this could be organised quickly enough to take over from UNO in the Congo and also help the Algerians).

3 A press conference to announce the formation of the union and to request the co-operation of the press. This was necessary because our protest rally was to be held at a place far removed from the centre of activity of those imperialists we sought to condemn. Unless the press and radio could make a lot of noise on our behalf our efforts would be entirely fruitless.

4 An evening party on Africa Day, April 15, 1961, to inaugurate the union.

5 A protest demonstration and mass rally to be held in
Peking city on Sunday, April 16, to protest against
the assassination of Lumumba and demand that the
colonialists quit Africa immediately.

The program was ambitious and we could never have
planned it on so grand a scale but for the financial and
material aid promised by the Chinese. In all, the union
spent only about 165 yuan in the preparation of banners
and placards and other minor items. The Chinese took
care of everything else, spending altogether about
1,000 yuan on the project. It was clear that we were to
share the benefits two ways: we on our side were cele-
brating Africa Day the way we ourselves planned and
wanted; the Chinese on their side were reaping the
propaganda value of our rally: it was anti-imperialist.

After dispatching the two cables in the morning of
Friday, April 14, we held our press conference in the
afternoon. Peking then had many foreign journalists
who had come to cover the international table tennis
championships and forty-two of them accepted our
invitation. The first three items on our celebration
program thus went off without a hitch, but not so the
fourth and fifth. The Somali students among us had
earlier submitted that April 15 was the birthday
anniversary of their party and that they would like to
make a speech to celebrate the occasion on our inauguration night. We agreed. Though we were not all
that clear about our attitude to individual African
political parties, we couldn't very well have refused them
the chance to speak. But when they decided to carry
placards denouncing Emperor Haile Selassie as an imperialist, we resisted because we were not clear about
the Somalia-Ethiopia border question and were not
prepared to commit the union blindly; moreover, we did

not think it proper that Africans should start by exposing their domestic quarrels in a foreign country on their very first outing. The Somalis were not satisfied, and for that reason refused to deliver their speech on inauguration day or to take part in either the demonstration or the rally. These Somalis brought up the idea of 'black imperialism' at a time when the minds of other Africans were completely unprepared to receive it. Those were times when we still thought, like many Africans today, that an imperialist must necessarily be white and foreign, must possess colonies and actively control or seek to control the economy of another country. We certainly could not believe that an imperialist can be black and your next-door neighbour who, just yesterday, was also groaning under the yoke of colonialism.

Our inauguration party was a great success. We had the UAR ambassador and representatives of the embassies of Ghana and Congo (Gizenga). Besides them many important Chinese organisations were also represented. It was at this function that both the embassies of Ghana and the UAR gave unsolicited financial aid to the new-born union. The Ghana embassy donated 500 yuan (over £70) and promised 500 yuan more if we could form a union of all Africans in China (as opposed to a union of students only). The UAR embassy donated 1,000 yuan (about £143) with no conditions attached.

I must say a few things about these donations. They certainly relieved a sore need, because our own finances were highly inadequate. I reasoned at that time (and subsequent events proved me right), that without much money our union would be subject to almost total Chinese control. Whenever we had a project, such as the anti-imperialist demonstration, which the Chinese thought could benefit them, their money would be freely available to finance it, but when they thought a project of ours would exclusively benefit the Africans, there would be no funds forthcoming from them. We would then be forced to think only in terms of things likely to meet with Chinese approval. But then, our major aim was not to aid China but rather to aid the African liberation struggle. We had made it clear in very strong terms from the very beginning that our union was not prepared to accept control or to toe the Communist Party line in any way. It was this which caused our officers to reject the red banners the Chinese had made for us to carry at the demonstration. We weren't running the risk of being dubbed 'red', I told them. We would carry only white banners. We did just that.

Another point about the financial aid: whereas it appeared that the donation of 500 yuan from Ghana came as a result of well-considered thought, the UAR donation was made entirely on the spur of the moment. Ghana spoilt her case by offering a further 500 yuan to be paid only on the fulfilment of certain specified conditions, *i.e.*, the formation of an All-African Union in China. Such a union, I must admit, was highly desirable, but the monetary inducement offered beforehand amounted to a political string which many of the students resented. The promised sum of 500 yuan, by the way, was never collected because the All-African Union was never formed. Ghana's actual donation of 500 yuan was also withdrawn a year later for unspecified reasons.

Sunday, April 16, was the demonstration and rally day. Under a formidable forest of placards and banners condemning imperialism (we meant Western), old and neo-colonialism, supporting African unity, lamenting Lumumba's murder and crying death to his assassins, and generally expressing in the most passionate and vehement

terms the same sentiments one would expect from any
African nationalists at that stage of our struggle, we
marched along Peking's main street running in front of
the Gate of Heavenly Peace. But there was one striking
point: though we praised our African leaders to the skies,
we scrupulously avoided mentioning the name of, or
laying emphasis on, any one of them. We considered that
each one was contributing in his own way to Africa's
liberation and unity. To single out just one or a few could
only give rise to jealousy. This wise precaution is sadly
lacking in the politics of our continent today, and I
believe that it is one of the factors that are making our
struggle towards African unity so painfully difficult.

Our Students' Union represented seven African nationalities when we started. We were spared a great deal of
useless bickering by the fact that our leadership came
from the minority groups only: Uganda (with four
students only) gave us our President, Ghana (also with
only four students) gave us our Secretary-General and
Chad (with just one student) gave us our Finance
Secretary. The result was that the officers were supported
entirely on their merits and not merely from national
considerations. Had they been elected from among the
more powerful nationalities (in point of numbers), the
smaller nationalities would have had almost no voice.
When it came to the time of actual election of officers,
however, some nationalities, acting like political parties,
had each decided which posts they wanted to retain for
themselves and just who from among them were to hold
such posts. We couldn't have avoided trouble under such
circumstances, and we had plenty of it, too. But in just
the same unwise manner some African leaders have
already shown in action, if not perhaps in speech, that
they consider themselves alone as qualified to lead a
united Africa. Since there are really several leaders with

the same high ambitions, it will be difficult for them to
agree to unite unless something gives somewhere. Until
tribalistic views and personal power ambitions are set
aside, African unity, even when finally achieved, will be
very unstable. I am not being merely pessimistic; this
unity is something I have worked for in my small way
in China, and I do hope for its success with all my heart.
But we do not succeed by concealing the ugly facts from
ourselves. The ostrich's enemies do not disappear merely
because that bird has hidden its head in the sand and
can no longer see those enemies. We must face up to the
realities and genuinely seek to overcome the difficulties.
This, and not altiloquent speeches, is the first realistic
step towards our cherished goal—African unity.

Now back to our demonstration and rally in Peking.
Marching with us that day were 3,000 Chinese students
besides a large number of European and Asian students;
in all the participation was nearly 4,000. At the rally,
which we held in an open-air theatre in Sun Yat Sen
Park, our three *ad hoc* officers and one Chinese comrade
were the speakers. In our speeches we told the American
imperialists and all other imperialists and colonialists to
go to hell and leave Africa alone (don't mind the language:
that was the mood). We touched on a great many subjects, from the Congo situation through the strife in
Angola to the Algerian war; from Apartheid through the
Ghana-Guinea-Mali Union and African unity to dis-
armament. The demonstration and rally were a grand
success, a very good beginning for our union. However,
all our precautions to the contrary did not prevent
sections of the Western press from calling us 'communist youth'. Such names did not worry us much any-
way; they were normally to be expected.

*   *   *

The Africa Week celebrations over, we settled down to the more sober work of drafting our constitution. With all seven nationalities represented on the constitutional committee and each representative asserting that his idea was better than anybody else's, work on the constitution was painfully slow. Our aims and objects are the only parts of the constitution that I think can interest outsiders. Of our aims the most salient (content not context) were:

(a) To bring African students in China together to learn unity by working in concert.

(b) To do whatever lay in our power to hasten the liberation of Africa from every kind of imperialist influence and to promote the cause of African unity.

(c) To help promote friendship and concord among the peace-loving nations of the world.

(d) To fight against all forms of discrimination.

We went to China at a time when the graph of African nationalism had reached one of its peaks, due to the Congo crisis—a time when it would have been considered positively unpatriotic of any enlightened African to remain aloof from the current political developments in the continent. It should be no surprise that we made African politics rather than other and tamer student interests our main aim. Besides, we were guests of a people so political that we really could not avoid catching the political fever. It was fortunate that we pointed our noses towards Africa rather than towards Karl Marx, much to the dismay of our Chinese hosts. We had China in mind, of course, when we wrote 'peace-loving nations'. We didn't then know as much as we knew later! Looking back, I now question the wisdom of promoting concord amongst peace-loving nations exclusively. If there is going to be trouble in the world, it will come from the non-peace-loving nations; and it is they, more than any one else, who need to be persuaded into the fold of those who 'seek peace and ensue it'.

Because the Chinese had always feared that, solidly united, we might come out with a whole barrage of demands for improvement in our social life, we scrupulously avoided any direct mention of social life in our constitution, though the question had always been uppermost in our minds. If, in later days, our union stood up to demand justice for an injured member and respect for our race and colour, it was entirely because the Chinese had pressed us to a point where we were prepared to act and be damned. (We were already committed to fight against racial discrimination any way.)

Before our constitution was completed, however, there was another important event that brought about much conflict and from which we learnt many another valuable lesson. That event was the visit of President Nkrumah to China. Ghana's leader was due in August when we were on vacation and arrangements for meeting him should have been easy were it not that many of the African students had qualms about the man himself. I shall begin that story from its very beginning to make it intelligible.

While the President was in Moscow, the Ghanaian ambassador in Peking went to meet him in the USSR. On the ambassador's return to Peking he made us understand that the President was prepared to buy us a club house, *provided that all Africans in Peking would unite*. A club in Peking exclusively for us Africans would be an extremely valuable asset. We had complained to African diplomatists and delegates on countless occasions of the miserable life we were leading, with no facilities for good entertainment. A club could go a very long way towards making our condition more tolerable. We did not doubt the truth of what the ambassador said, neither did we doubt him when he said that a similar thing had already been done for African residents in Moscow. (I unfortunately forgot to check up on this when I got to Moscow in April 1962.) If there was any trace of doubt it was quickly dispelled by the picture of Africa Unity House, the club costing about £54,000 (and named after Nkrumah's mother) which the President had donated to the Committee of African Organisations in London. The inducement of 500 yuan previously offered by the Ghanaian embassy to make us form an All-African union did not impress us. In actual fact we rejected it and clearly inscribed into our constitution a clause that we were only prepared to accept aid which came completely without strings. The club house donation, considered from every angle, also had strings attached. But I must confess that, considering the facts of China, the bribe was so big we never really remembered what we had inscribed in the constitution (not then approved, however). If that club offer was rejected in the long run, it was due to animosity towards Nkrumah's person and to suspicion of his intentions; certainly not to our high respect for the ideals of our own constitution.

From here on and for a while in my narration I shall have to substitute an 'I' for every 'we' since I was solely in charge of arrangements for the All-African Union.

The general attitude of the students indicated that they welcomed the idea of the club, but there were a few very wet blankets. At the first preparatory meeting I summoned, an objection was raised to the formation of the new union. This objection was based on the argument that, since the students already had a union and since the membership of the new union would be mainly student, there was no call for a new union. But the facts are that the students at that time numbered about eighty and the non-students about forty-three. Besides, the bigger All-African Union could have made it possible to admit four other African nationalities: Algeria, Mali, UAR and Sudan; states not represented in the Students' Union. I may mention, in passing, that the man who was the first to discourage the All-African Union was the very man who had paid us a visit on the occasion of our first representative conference to discuss final arrangements for the Students' Union. He had then spoken in favour of expanding the scope of the Union so as to enable non-students to join. This man was the leader of the Zanzibaris. He afterwards went over to the Chinese side against his own Zanzibari brethren and was promptly deposed from the leadership.

At a second preparatory meeting where the Ghanaian ambassador was present and addressed us, the proposal for the formation of the enlarged Union was rejected once and for all. I am not quite clear what happened behind the scenes but I was aware that there was much anti-Ghana propaganda, especially by some very influential embassies. A few things became clear to me afterwards, however, as I pieced together fragmentary information gathered during our conversations. Most of them believed that Ghana had an unexplained motive for wanting the formation of the All-African Union. The 500 yuan promised to the students *on condition* that the enlarged union was formed, and the club house offered to all of us *on condition* that the enlarged union was formed, both lent weight to the argument of an ulterior motive. Furthermore, the students were already well organised enough to argue: why not donate the club to the Students' Union, if the sole or main aim is to do a kind deed to relieve our suffering? But they were told flatly: no expanded union, no club house. If any previously did not

believe in an ulterior motive, this was reason enough to
make them change their mind. They did. There was
another point also. The majority thought that Ghana was
stealing the show too often.

The question, as I see it, goes deeper than these super-
ficialities. Those Africans were not merely against
Ghana's stealing the show too often. What is really
offensive to them (it still remains so to many Africans) is
the inordinate loudness with which Ghana blows her
own trumpet after stealing the show. Most people are
content to look up to a leader, but where that leader
always appears to want to emphasise the weakness and
incapability of his followers, they cannot help growing
resentful even if they are too small to rival him. This is
where some modesty counts. This is where the leader
stands to gain by saying less about his own and more
about the contributions of others. But Ghana's Convention People's Party, like the Chinese Communist
Party that it copies, does not appear to have any sense of
political modesty. It appears to think that Nkrumah
grows bigger in measure of the lofty titles conferred on
him. His zealots lack the elementary psychological in-
sight to realise that a title like 'King of Africa' is positively
offensive to other Africans, besides making ridiculous the
uncrowned man on whom it is conferred. When Achille
Starace, one-time Secretary of Mussolini's Fascist Party,
issued an order that everyone who wrote a letter in Italy
of that time should end it *Viva il Duce*, Mussolini had
the presence of mind, when he discovered it, to realise
that the order made him ridiculous before the whole of
Italy. Mussolini *was* absolute ruler of Italy then, but
even he thought *Viva il Duce* at the end of all letters
made him ridiculous. Nkrumah is only *aspiring* to be
leader of a united Africa. How much more ridiculous
must he not look to have assumed the title of 'King'

before his African 'subjects' have accepted him as such?

There is one other important lesson we can learn from the club-house case: the lesson that in the matter of African unity, it no longer pays to offer bribes (if we stop being prudish, an inducement with conditions is a bribe pure and simple). At the time when people had not clearly understood the need for unity, it paid to offer inducement to people to make them stop and listen, just as a bar-keeper, say, may play recorded music to attract customers to his beer. But what is the use of more bribes when the people have stopped, listened and are convinced of the need for unity? Our present difficulty is not *whether* we shall unite; no, that is already solved—we will; our difficulty now is *how* we shall unite. To continue offering bribes at a time when the question remaining is only 'how we shall unite', can really make people suspect that the one offering the bribes wants us to unite the way *he* chooses. And the way Ghana can choose (no free press, no freedom of speech, spies and detention cells and all that) is not necessarily the way all Africans are going to like. So by pressing ahead too far, too fast (Chinese style), Ghana is actually hindering instead of helping the cause of African unity.

We cannot build a stable union by buying, that is to say bribing, people into it. Today you pay a man black-mail to keep a thing secret, tomorrow he is going to set his tongue wagging fast unless you can afford more black-mail. Today you pay a man to support you. You have made him learn how 'sweet' easy money is. Tomorrow he may support that other opponent over there who can pay a heavier bribe than you. You have corrupted that man. In future he will offer his support, not according to his conscience and the merits of the case, but according to the most attractive inducement offered him.

The African residents in Peking rejected President

Nkrumah's club-house though it could have been the
one single thing that could have held some of them back
in China when poor conditions had already made them
decide to leave. It was then that I realised most clearly
how very unpopular Ghana and her Nkrumah had
grown.

This was the background to President Nkrumah's visit.
As you can imagine, it was no easy job to prepare for it.
And there were serious administrative difficulties. Of
the three *ad hoc* officers, our President, Okidi, had left
for Africa. He and the other five Ugandans and Kenyans
were fed up with China. Our Finance Secretary had gone
to Moscow, intentionally locking the Union's funds in the
bank meanwhile. I had to dig into my slender pocket to
pay for all the banners and placards and the bouquet we
carried. (When it all ended I went off on a delayed visit
to North Korea with literally not a cent in my pocket. I
must say it to the credit of the Korean Youth League, my
hosts in that country, that, despite my financial handicap, I
never wanted for food, drink, smokes and services.)
But the thing was done in the end. There was, however, a
small hitch in our arrangements. A great many students
refused to sing the song: 'There is victory for us, in the
struggle of Africa there_ is victory. Forward ever,
Backward never . . .', suggested by the Ghanaian embassy.
This song, by the way, was the battle song of Ghana's
Convention People's Party; only 'Africa' has been substituted for 'CPP'. It has been sung at many international
political conferences held in Accra, much to the annoyance of some participants who knew its origin. The
students saw in this yet another attempt by Ghana to
ram too many things down everybody's throat. Still, I
persuaded them finally to learn it at the very last
moment—on the bus on our way to the airport. It will

not escape my readers' notice that, paradoxically, it was I who was doing the throat-ramming in getting them to sing the song of the CPP, a party with whom I have always been at logger-heads. But I was proud of my President, though I disliked much of his politics. And, in any case, as Secretary-General of the Union, I would have exerted myself no less for any other visiting African dignitary.

In drizzling rain, our clothes soaked almost to the skin, our banners and placards ruined, we nevertheless sang 'There is victory for us' to the accompaniment of a trumpet and a saxophone—sang it like mad—to welcome Nkrumah, President of the Republic of Ghana.

*　　　*　　　*

I shall not bother my readers with an account of the election which succeeded the completion of our constitution. Suffice it to mention that high officials of the Chinese government working through one of their collaborators among us, a man called Nyobe, bluntly gave us to understand that they would be intensely displeased if some eight particular Camerounian students were elected to office. Those eight, they said, were known to be American spies. What nonsense! Can anyone imagine the Chinese knowing of an American spy in their midst and not eliminating him? But they succeeded in their object; they widened an already existing split. Our unity was a threat to them; they made that clear to us, though not in so many words, from the very beginning. To avert that threat they had either to make the Union work entirely as they wanted by dominating or tricking its officers, or else cause such a wide rift as to wreck the Union entirely. In the latter case they could always blame everything on our own ineptitude.

One such case of trickery occurred in February 1962.

I had temporarily resigned my post as Secretary-General and the Chinese saw in that a chance to get just what they wanted. There was some disagreement among us at this time, and, for that reason, we had not made any arrangements for commemorating the anniversary of Lumumba's assassination.

The Chinese, however, made elaborate arrangements for the anniversary celebration, bringing in a big truck with recording equipment for the occasion. The queer thing was that the very members of the Union's Central Committee who should have taken the decision and made the arrangements in the first place, did not know anything about the celebration till about one hour before it was due to start. And that celebration had been arranged *in the name of our Union*. It was no surprise to me that many committee members exploded. It was not that they saw anything wrong in commemorating Lumumba's assassination. No, Lumumba was our hero and will remain so for always. But the fact was that the Chinese were using our Union to gain their own ends. The Congo's withdrawal of her diplomatic mission from China was a great blow to the Chinese as well as to the whole of the communist bloc, which had specific and unholy designs on that part of Africa. What the Chinese were doing was to use us to recoup some of their losses, to save face, and to make Africa believe that the Chinese actually love the Congo.

I was away from Peking in February 1961 when the monster rally was held in the Workers' Stadium to protest against Lumumba's murder, but I have since witnessed several other similar rallies and, what is more, I have learnt how they are organised. The Party orders that it wants fifty, seventy or a hundred thousand persons to attend such-and-such a rally; and the heads of street committees, factories and other establishments select the people who are to attend. When you are selected, attendance is compulsory, but when you are not selected you have no right to attend. Each group of participants is under an individual who alone is authorised to act as slogan-leader, the slogans being approved by the Party for the occasion. The same standard banners were used at almost all the rallies in which I participated, though the objects of the rallies differed widely. At the rally you watch your group leader and applaud when he does, shout when he does. In the whole show there is not a single trace of that spontaneity which should mark the public demonstration of people who, moved by a common sentiment, rally together to put that sentiment into words and action. One might easily ask: of the thousands who were herded into the Peking Workers' Stadium to protest against Lumumba's murder, how many were sincere? And above all, if they had not been forced to attend that rally, how many would have come of their own free will?

Thus, with rigged rallies and protest marches, the Chinese Communist Party manages to deceive us Africans into believing that the Chinese people are solidly behind us. What hypocrisy! What abject insincerity!

I hardly need mention that this Chinese attempt to make our Union their instrument promptly brought me back to my post. What the pleas of my African fellows could not do the Chinese did, though the results were not at all to their liking.

F

12

The Ali Affair

Now to the final episode in this history of the African Students' Union in China: the events in late March 1962. I was at that time the sole African student in Peking Medical College, and I used to while away my more lonely moments in telephone conversations with African friends at the Language Institute. One Wednesday morning, in the course of such a conversation with a member of our Central Committee, I was told there had been a brawl in the city involving one of the Zanzibari students. I was not made to understand that it was anything serious. The following day I got all the details, from which it appeared it was very serious indeed.

A young Zanzibari called Ali had gone with a Mongol friend to the Peace Hotel. While there, Ali went to the counter to buy some cigarettes, but was refused by the man at the counter. As they stood arguing, two hotel stewards came out and laid hands on Ali. They did not turn him out of the hotel, as is usually done with people who, rightly or wrongly, are regarded as nuisances; no, they hauled him off to an adjoining room and started to beat him up. Ali fought back manfully but more Chinese stewards rushed in and pitched into him, dragging him into the yard outside.

At that time there were two other Zanzibaris present in the hotel, a man and his wife, both working at Radio Peking. The woman was seven months' pregnant.

Hearing the row that was being kicked up, they went, out of curiosity, to see what it was all about. As soon as they showed their faces, the Chinese fell on them also. Ever since the assault on Ali began, this mob of toughs had been yelling: '*Fei chou ren bu hao*'—Africans are not good. Since Ali had done or said something which, to their mind, merited a beating, they considered it logical to deal out similar treatment to every African in sight. *All* Africans were 'not good'. They weren't content with using their fists. The spittoon-covers in Chinese hotels are large disks with longish handles. When wielded as a club, these covers can be as effective as a Zulu warrior's knob-kerrie. The African woman was beaten with them till she sustained injuries on the breast and other parts of the body. Ali fainted and dropped to the floor, where his body was a target for anyone's boot.

There was a burly black-bearded West Indian staying at the hotel called John Holmes. He had been in Peking for about eighteen months and had been friendly with the African students. He had helped the Union's officers to patch up the split which developed when the Somalis wanted to carry anti-Ethiopian posters in the demonstration. Hearing the hullabaloo, Mr Holmes came down from the eighth floor, sized up the situation, and carried Ali's limp form up to his own apartment and gave him first aid.

But when he tried to convey Ali and the injured pregnant woman to hospital, the hotel lift suddenly decided to go out of order and no taxis were to be got for love or money in all Peking. You can't just go to the curb and hail a taxi in Peking; you have to telephone to the taxi-office and then sit and wait for one to arrive; sometimes it takes a whole hour, if you are lucky! If the caller happens not to be in the good books of the authorities, he can wait till he is blue in the face, but no taxi will arrive. Nor did it arrive in this case. The Chinese were clearly not satisfied with merely giving three 'niggers' a good beating. There was to be no transport to take them to hospital. It was not until about four o'clock in the morning, that is *eight* hours after the assault, that the injured were finally taken away for treatment. And this was only due to the fact that their Zanzibari friends found transport for them.

Mr Holmes was disgusted and said he would 'quit this bloody country' if justice were not done to the injured Africans. He belonged, so he told me, to the Committee of African Organisations in London. Some people said he was a communist. If this is so, then I take my hat off to him, for he would then be that very rare specimen, a communist who puts justice above the Party. Because he spoke out in indignation and demanded 'justice to the injured or I quit', he was promptly accused of inciting the Africans to action. The Chinese told him he would be held responsible for any retaliatory action we students took as a result of the Ali Affair. A few days before I left China I heard that he was also packing up to leave.

The African woman involved in this appalling incident was, as I have said, employed by Radio Peking. She was an announcer on the Swahili language program. Not long before the incident, it had been part of her job to tell East Africans the story of a pregnant woman in South Korea who had been beaten up by an American sailor. The story was broadcast to show American brutality to less favoured peoples. And now she who told the story was being assaulted, not by one drunken man, but by a whole crowd of sober ruffians, beaten up by Chinese merely because she was African.

No wonder the Chinese tried to persuade us African students to keep quiet about the affair! What price Sino-African friendship now?

When the Africans at the Language Institute heard about the affair, they exploded. I found them seething with rage and demanding that the matter be placed forthwith on the agenda of the Union's meeting scheduled for Sunday, March 25. They demanded a strike— a one-week hunger strike: everyone was to down tools and go without food for a week. In these circumstances, the general meeting was bound to be stormy. Accordingly, I consulted with Mr Kassim, our President (a Zanzibari), and we agreed it was advisable to call a meeting of the Central Committee on Saturday, March 24. In the less turbulent atmosphere of the committee meeting, it might be possible to make some constructive proposals to calm down our fellow students and at the same time deal with the Chinese.

The Committee meeting started at four in the afternoon. Business had just started when a number of dignitaries turned up. These were the ambassadors of the Republic of Guinea with another diplomatist from that embassy, the ambassador of the Republic of Mali with an embassy counsellor, and the *chargé d'affaires* of the Ghanaian embassy. This was the first time we had received such an impressive delegation, but I must confess that we were less enthusiastic than we would ordinarily have been. We were too conscious of what our fellow students would do by way of direct action if they failed to be satisfied with the measures proposed by the Central Committee. The two ambassadors went aside to speak to individual students, mainly the Camerounians with whom they could speak French. The other three diplomatists came over to confer with the Central Committee, trying hard to persuade us to cancel the meeting of the whole Union fixed for the following day. They feared this meeting would lead to the students' taking action which might bring further trouble. But they made an unfortunate, and very undiplomatic, mistake: they started by telling us we were in the wrong. When a group of hotheads have risen up in holy anger and are on the warpath, no one can start off like that without raising more hell. Things were made worse when we discovered that they had heard the Chinese story, ready cooked for consumption, without bothering to get from Ali his version of the case. (I should make it clear that the ambassadors themselves did not take part in these direct discussions with the Committee. Things might have taken a different turn if they had.) Ali might well have been in the wrong, but should this be assumed automatically, and should he be condemned without a hearing? The fact is, these diplomatists came at the instance of the Chinese Foreign Ministry; they had not come to arbitrate in the dispute with the Chinese, but to get us to do what the Chinese wanted. The upshot was that we told them we could not agree there and then to their request to cancel the meeting next day, but would consider it during our deliberations on the whole affair. They left at about seven o'clock.

After a break, the Committee met again from ten o'clock to three in the morning. We considered the advice given by the diplomatists and in the end decided to ignore it for the following reasons:

1 The advice came, not from them, but from the Chinese since the diplomatists were simply acting as emissaries of the Chinese.

2 The diplomatists were not objective, showing partiality in all respects to the Chinese case.

3 We were at loggerheads with the Chinese in a local matter. There was no cause to raise it to the status of an international dispute, as was implicit in the intervention of three embassies.

4 The general meeting of the Union had been fixed
two weeks earlier to deal with matters of internal
discipline. We didn't intend to change our plans
just to please the Chinese who had provoked trouble
by beating up our friends.

5 Collective opinion in the Union was firmly against
cancelling the Sunday meeting. If the Central
Committee could not retain members' confidence,
the students might well break loose from all
control.

6 Union officers believed that, somehow or other, they
could keep effective control of the situation. But to
do so, they had to meet the whole body of students.
The officers would be abdicating responsibility if
they cancelled the meeting.

The strength of feeling among the students can be
judged by the reaction of some of the Camerounian
girls when I jokingly said, before going into the second
session of the Committee meeting, that the general
meeting was to be postponed on Chinese advice. Four or
five of them flew at me in fury and it would have gone
ill with me if I hadn't quickly told them I was pulling
their legs.

So, in the early hours of the morning it was decided
that the general meeting should still take place.

*   *   *

That same Saturday night two other events occurred
which deserve mention. There was a group amongst us
which did not appear to have definite ideas of their own.
These were the 'drifters'. On several occasions the
Chinese had used these to put rifts among us. With a
view to breaking student solidarity over the Ali case,

the Chinese invited all the Somali students and a large
section of the Camerounians to two different parties that
evening. The Zanzibaris, Ghanaians and the intractable
group among the Camerounians were not invited. At
Sino-African Friendship House, the Chinese spent four
hours trying to persuade the Somalis to dissociate themselves from any action proposed by the Union. But the
sweet talk and all the wines and delicacies did not make
any impression on the Somalis. On the contrary, they
poured out to the Chinese all their grievances and reported back to the Central Committee. At a similar party
on the premises of the Afro-Asian Solidarity Committee,
the Chinese had no better luck with the Camerounians,
who told them quite bluntly how miserable their lives
were being made in China. No one had instructed these
two groups how to behave towards the Chinese; despite
all differences in the past, they rallied to the viewpoint
of the majority of their fellow Africans. Chinese efforts
to split us only resulted in a greater unity amongst the
African students, a solidarity which overcame the petty
jealousies and differences which had earlier afflicted the
Union.

In the Language Institute the same night the Chinese
were holding a dance party to celebrate the Algerian cease
fire. We Africans had previously discussed giving a party,
but we finally decided against it because the atmosphere
at the time was not favourable for hilarious celebrations.
We therefore decided to send a congratulatory letter to
the Provisional Government instead. This party of the
Chinese, I must explain, was not at all the good-will-and-
solidarity-with-Algerians affair that you would think. It
was solely for propaganda. The major preoccupation of
most Chinese officials—teachers, party officials and students alike—at that period was to prevent us from holding

a general meeting on Sunday morning. Individual contacts with African students in all the colleges and universities, the dispatching of African diplomatists as
emissaries, banquets at the Sino-African Friendship
Association and the Afro-Asian Solidarity Committee,
the dance party at the Language Institute—all were
major links in the chain of efforts to stop us from holding
our scheduled meeting.

It happened that I was one of a handful of African
students who went to the dance hall. The other students
had secretly passed the word round, without the Committee's knowledge, that the dance was to be boycotted.
It was only a few Somalis who had not heard about the
boycott who attended it for a brief space. My purpose
there was to look for the Vice-President of our Union,
who had not shown up by the time our Committee
meeting was about to open at 10 p.m. There was an
impressive turn-out of prominent members of the
Language Institute and Medical College, leading figures
of the Communist Party and the Youth League. You
should have been there to see the obsequious attentions
with which I was received. The manner in which the
Chinese vied with each other as to who would hug me
most closely, and who give me the broadest smiles, was
positively revolting. It was by no means through chance
that the Chinese took such a great interest in me that
night. (Former lecturers of mine suddenly expressed
their readiness to prepare a bed for me if I intended to
spend the night at the Institute.) I was an officer of the
Union and known to have a good deal of personal as well
as official influence with my fellow Africans. The
Chinese were hoping to induce me to use this influence
to cancel or postpone the general meeting. They failed.

If there was little sleep for our Central Committee
that night, there was none for the 'comrades'. The dance

party ruse had turned out a flop, the efforts to split the students had failed. They had to spend the rest of the night thinking out how best to deal with their rebellious black comrades.

13

Sunday, March 25

Sunday morning came at last and at ten o'clock the African students presented themselves at the meeting in full force. In feverish expectancy they listened while the officers cautioned them to behave their best in order to put to shame all those who refused to credit us with any higher intelligence than that of suckling babes. There were only two items on the agenda: (a) internal discipline and (b) other matters. Internal discipline was placed with intent to divert their attention from the more pressing matter of the Ali Assault Case. To explain the item 'internal discipline' I must make a longish but necessary digression.

As in any large group of people, there were students among us whose behaviour left much to be desired. It was our purpose to single out the different kinds of acts of misbehaviour which could tarnish the good reputation of Africans, and to take measures to prevent repetitions.

Foreign students, I have mentioned earlier, were not subject to any limitations in the amount of food, drink, smokes, and also in the beginning, clothing. Though our supply of cloth was theoretically unlimited, we required cloth coupons; these were supplied by the Foreign Students' Office on demand. Many of us had no qualms at all about giving a packet of cigarettes or a plate of rice and stew to a *bona fide* Chinese friend, though we knew the authorities did not like it. We found it difficult to understand why a friend who had travelled several miles from the city to visit us at the campus should be left without lunch. Such things were not in our book, coming as we did from a continent where, in spite of our 'primitiveness', we have managed not to be too mean about food. Accordingly, regulations or no regulations, we let our friends partake freely of what we had. Occasional cloth coupons also went to girl friends without any pricks of conscience. But the majority of us were rudely shocked when we learnt that a few of us were actually selling cigarettes and cloth coupons to Chinese at black market prices. Such a practice, quite apart from soiling the reputation of us all, could affect us more directly by causing the authorities to effect a drastic cut in our supplies. Selling cigarettes and cloth coupons for profit had to be stopped at once.

I will not defend such people for a bit, but I must say in fairness to them that they were driven to it. The dreariness of our life made some students want to buy things like transistor radios and gramophone record players which really went a long way towards relieving our mental tension. But to buy such things you need money. The 100 yuan a month was hardly enough to cater for necessities, much less for luxuries. So the more unscrupulous resorted to shady methods they had learnt from the '*Húa qiáo*' — Overseas Chinese.

These Overseas Chinese were lured from many different parts, mainly Indonesia, and came to settle, they thought, in a Fatherland overflowing with milk and honey. Most unfortunately, however, they met only with hunger and destitution where they expected plenty. Since they were mainly relatives of wealthy Overseas Chinese and were used to luxurious living, life in China was to them such intolerable torture that they tried many crooked means of obtaining necessities that they

would not otherwise have. I was walking in the city one
winter night when one of them accosted me and, with no
preliminaries whatever, requested me to help him pur-
chase some cotton padding for his winter coat. The store
he described was open only to foreigners and the bosses.
When I refused to help him, arguing that as an officer
of our Union I was the last person to do a forbidden thing
like that, he stuck to me like a leach, offering me higher
and higher monetary inducements. I had quite a task of
it shaking that chap off. On another occasion another
man, a full-blooded Chinese this time, approached me,
touched the green sweater I was wearing and pointed
to the department store: would I help him to buy a
sweater? He was feeling terribly cold; foreigners didn't
need coupons for sweaters. With that he held out a roll
of bank notes. It was hard to refuse, seeing the man's
condition, but I did refuse. Hard-hearted? No. It was just
'against the rules', and if I was going to make other students
obey the rules I had to start by obeying them myself
even when no one was looking. When I caught up with
the two companions with whom I was walking when the
man hailed me, they chided me roundly for refusing to
help him. It was to such temptations that we were daily
exposed. Listening to these piteous pleas, a man must be
really hard to resist. I do not relate these to show how
good I was and how obedient to rules. In fact I was not
much better than the common run and did not always
live up to my high ideals. I gave cigarettes and food to
friends too; but always free of charge. But even that was
not allowed.

Another burning question was that of girl friends.
Boy-meets-girl affairs are perfectly permissible in China
granting Chinese boy and Chinese girl or European boy
and Chinese girl, but where it is African boy trying to
meet Chinese girl then there is a whole lot of noise and

fuss all over the place. I have to explain that Chinese
girls sought foreigners for reasons quite different from
those that impelled foreigners to seek Chinese. Through
association with foreigners, Chinese girls assured for
themselves extra cloth coupons as well as extra food.
Visiting their foreign friends they could eat meat and
eggs and drink milk, things they had not tasted for long
periods. Probably the strongest of all their reasons was
that they wanted to get married. Their reasoning was
simple: they desperately wanted to clear out of China.

Marrying a foreign student was an almost foolproof
way of clearing out. I was having a casual talk with a girl
in Peking one day when she told me that after her
college training she would be receiving 43 yuan (a little
more than £6) a month. When I mentioned to her that
with her training she would be receiving something
around £60 (roughly 420 yuan) a month in the outside
world, she couldn't believe her ears. She asked to marry
me all the same. Unfortunately for her I was already
married. That was my second marriage proposal from
Chinese girls. They wouldn't wait for you to propose,
they did the proposing. I could cite dozens of other
instances of African students' receiving similar proposals.
It was no pleasure to watch how bitterly some of them
wept when they learnt they had no chance. There were
students among us who seriously wanted to get married,
however. We had heard that about ten of the Camerounian students in Moscow had already got married to Mosco-
vites. Why couldn't we do the same in Peking? It was
only a few days to the date of my departure that I learnt
the answer. The Party does not allow marriage between
Chinese women and foreign men, I was told by Chen
Yu, a member of the People's Congress. But I knew a
European student in Peking University who married a
Chinese. There was a coloured student in the People's

University who had married a Chinese. The latter man's case is rather peculiar, of course. What I learnt about him was that he was one of the American soldiers taken prisoner during the Korean War. This Afro-American refused to go home and is now studying philosophy or something of the sort in that university. In his case the Chinese could not well have refused him a wife since he would have found it difficult to import one.

In view of these facts it is difficult to discover whether the Chinese really do not want inter-marriage or whether they invented that rule solely to block any serious amorous advances by Africans. Whatever the truth was, the Chinese helped precisely nobody when they packed all girl friends off to prison. Relations between the authorities and us became more strained than ever. In our attempt to normalise the situation, the Central Committee hoped to curb the ardour of those who were too bold with the girls. In short, we suggested in almost as many words that the boy-meets-girl affair should become an underground activity, since living in China for seven years without our normal share of fun was quite out of the question. The girl friend headache was not confined to us students. On Christmas Eve 1961, I met a strikingly pretty Chinese woman at a party in the apartment of a non-European diplomatist. Later on I learned she had been arrested and taken to an unknown destination.

Acting on behalf of the Central Committee, I made a lengthy speech on internal discipline, ending with a motion calling for strong condemnation of 'the activities of all students who, through various unpleasant acts, do offend the Chinese system and laws'. The motion was carried by 52 votes to 2 with only one abstention. That was a big victory for the Central Committee, but it is worth noting that when I had placed this same internal discipline on the agenda for two consecutive previous meetings, the Union would not allow its discussion. We were then too divided for them to want to be seriously disciplined, particularly by me. There was always an undercurrent of resentment against me. I came from Nkrumah's country.

With the end of discussions on internal discipline, the meeting also should have ended. That was the original plan of the secretariat and that would have been the case had the Chinese not thrust troubles upon us. The Ali case had to come. And it came—under 'other matters'.

I outlined the course of events since the evening when Ali and the other fellow Africans received the brutal treatment at the hands of the Chinese. The Central Committee's recommendation, I stressed, was that the matter could not be effectively dealt with by declaring a hunger and non-co-operation strike from the very outset. We had first to submit our grievances to the authorities, embarking on further action only if nothing or not enough was done to meet our demands. They didn't seem convinced and, as if to prove it, the Zanzibari and Camerounian students promptly submitted a resolution each. * Both resolutions went over our grievances and then suggested corrective measures. But whereas the more restrained Camerounian resolution recommended a Union delegation to meet and hold discussions with the Chinese, the more radical Zanzibari resolution asked for an immediate hunger and non-co-operation strike as a prelude to the discussions. After a lengthy and hot debate, the Central Committee on the one side urging moderation and the rank and file on the other side urging 'no softness or compromise', we finally agreed to delegate our Central Committee to meet the Chinese. The much-

* See appendices I and II.

feared trouble had been averted. It could have remained permanently averted but for the 'excessive
wisdom' of our Chinese hosts.

That afternoon, the Vice-Secretary-General and I
met the dean of the Language Institute and asked for an
appointment with representatives of the Ministry of
Education, the Sino-African Friendship Association,
the Afro-Asian Solidarity Committee, the All-China
Federation of Youth, the Peking Students' Union, the
All-China Federation of Women and the All-China
Federation of Labour. We wished to meet representatives
of some of these organisations because we held our
scholarships from them, and of other organisations
because they had solved certain of our problems in the
past. After some preliminary evasive tactics, the dean
agreed to arrange the meeting. We learned later in the
day that it was to take place on Monday morning at
nine o'clock.

All students went calmly about their daily business.
On the Central Committee's advice, they had agreed at
the general meeting to attend classes regularly the
following week. The barbaric acts the Chinese had led
our African diplomatists to expect from African students
did not materialise. We had proved more 'civilised' than
they had supposed. But the trouble was by no means
settled.

14

Monday, March 26

Monday morning came and, in a car provided by the Chinese, I reached the premises of the Afro-Asian Solidarity Committee, the meeting place of the proposed Sino-African conference. Disturbing news awaited me. I was told that my colleagues of the Central Committee (all in the Language Institute) had refused to attend the conference. My first thought was that they had let me down. I immediately telephoned the Institute, and was told they had, after all, left for the conference ten minutes earlier. It was not till they finally arrived that I got to know the truth. Early that morning the Chinese had told them that they wanted to meet the whole of the African student-body and not the Committee alone. This was a surprise to us because it was we who asked for the interview, specifying our Central Committee as our accredited representatives. The other students of course refused to attend the conference on Chinese invitation, arguing that they could not go back on a Union decision. The Chinese tried all their usual ruses. For example, they went to, say, the Somalis, and told them: 'Look, all the Camerounian students have agreed to go to the conference; they are already in the bus waiting for you.' Next they hurried to the Camerounians and told them the same thing of the Somalis. But this sort of dodge did not work. The students all replied that they were waiting for a positive order from the Central Committee, without which they were not prepared to move. They stayed behind.

The Chinese attached very great importance to this meeting. Two, and very possibly four, of the Chinese representatives were members of the Central Committee of the Communist Party. Another delegate was introduced as the Mayor of Peking. The leader of the Chinese delegation was a nasty bully who had returned from Africa a few days previously.

In the conference room Africans and Chinese were arguing back and forth about the attendance of the student-body. The Africans argued that: first it was they who had requested the meeting to which the Union had specifically sent its Central Committee as authorised representative; and secondly too many participants could bring trouble since the majority of the students was still in an ugly mood.

The Chinese were not impressed by our reasoning. They argued that, since we all held our scholarships from them, they had every right to demand to meet all of us any time they chose, and that, moreover, they were not aware that our Union had a committee of officers. This fruitless argument lasted three hours. Our Union President, Mr Kassim of Zanzibar, proposed that the meeting be called off, as nothing good could be expected to come out of it. This gave the Chinese a good chance to start the game at which they are adept: hunting for the scape-goat. If ever anything goes wrong in the relations between Chinese and foreigner, it must always be the foreigner that is at fault, never the Chinese. They immediately accused us of sabotaging the meeting by our intention to withdraw. It was when I tried to support our President's viewpoint that I made the comparison that set the cat among the pigeons. I told the Chinese that the Summit Conference, due to be held in Paris,

had to be called off because the sending of the U-2
spy plane by the United States to the USSR destroyed the
peaceful atmosphere in which alone any useful negotiations could have been held. Since the atmosphere at our
conference was not conducive to fruitful deliberation, it
was much better to call it off till we all had time to cool
down and think things over. The Chinese flew (or
pretended to fly) into a rage. Why should I compare them
to the American imperialists? they angrily demanded. I
went on to explain that I was by no means comparing one
people to another but rather the *atmosphere* at the
Summit to the *atmosphere* at our conference. (You are
now in a position to understand fully what I said about
the comparison of *attitudes* much earlier in this book.
That the U-2 incident might merely have supplied a
convenient pretext to quarters that did not want the
Summit to succeed in the first place, does not touch my
argument at all.) For no other reason than to help re-
introduce a little calm, I withdrew that comparison on
my own initiative *and* apologised, though to this day I
am not convinced that my comparison was wrong. The
upshot of our three-hour debate was that we agreed to
let all the students attend the conference. We knew
very well that all that the Chinese craved for was the
chance to say: 'When we (Chinese) wanted to settle the
dispute, you (Africans) wrecked our efforts.' We decided
not to give them that chance. Consent was wrested from
us by massive pressure.

While our conference was in progress, the Chinese
comrades were engaged in an interesting sideline
activity quite unknown to us. They had succeeded in
rounding up a number of African students from Peking
University, the People's University and the College of
Hydraulics. These students were given the impression
that all their fellows of the Language Institute were

already at the conference. While our talks were going on, these other Africans were also having discussions, presumably a much friendlier chat than our heated argument, with Chinese in another room. I cite this because it had a very important influence on the course of events. Among those secretly brought in were three students, Nyobe and Muzong of Cameroun and Abdallah of Chad. These three were very good friends of the Chinese and had consistently sided with them. Muzong and Abdallah belonged in one class—not at all intelligent in look but always toeing the Chinese line because, as they themselves said, they aspired to admission to the Chinese Communist Party. Muzong was so well known in Peking University as a Chinese collaborator that he hadn't a single friend among the foreign students of more than thirty different non-African nationalities. He faithfully reported to his bosses any private conversation he had with anyone.

Nyobe is quite a different character. He is an intelligent fellow and a good schemer who has always been at loggerheads both with our Union and with the Camerounian political party (UPC) that sponsored him. From him the Chinese learnt all that went on in our Union (though we had really no secrets), all that went on in the party meetings of the Camerounians and about everybody's private affairs. Before our general election of officers he met me secretly and said he would campaign for me to become President if only I could help him take my place as Secretary-General. I was prepared to serve the Union in any capacity if they had confidence in me, but I was not interested in campaigning for any particular post. I told him so, and he went away in disappointment to campaign elsewhere against me and my country. It was precisely this evil campaign and some other factors that had made me resign my post the very day I was re-elected Secretary-General. Again it was this Nyobe who stood up at our election meeting and told us all that he had first-hand information from some Chinese state ministers that they would be very displeased if some particular Camerounian students were elected officers. He was a veritable thorn in our side.

When the Chinese negotiators insisted upon meeting the whole student body, it was on these three, Nyobe, Muzong and Abdallah, that they relied for support. Among the Central Committee they had no supporters, but among the student-body they had at least our three black sheep. So they invited us all and trouble started in dead earnest.

While we waited for the rest of the students to arrive we began to discuss with the Chinese at their request the first item on our agenda. It was headed: 'Our faults.' We were being realistic; the faults could not lie entirely on one side. We had our faults too and it seemed a good point to detail these and let the comrades know what corrective measures we had taken or intended to take. This, we considered, would help the Chinese to understand that we sought justice and not only our own interests. Acting as the Committee's spokesman I gave the Chinese the same details about the misbehaviour of some of our number and the disciplinary measures we had taken so far. These details I have already given. We had just finished discussion on this when the other students arrived and the enlarged conference opened.

At the opening I gave our fellow students a very brief idea of what had transpired before their arrival and what led to their coming at all. Here I made a mistake. My account was too sketchy. I thus gave the Chinese the good chance of filling in the blanks from their imagination—to their own advantage, of course. But luckily I was there to retort and point out their falsehoods.

The first item on our list of grievances was racial discrimination. The opening sentence in my notes on the subject was: 'Many of the things that are done to African students and of which they daily complain can be embodied in the concept of the colour discrimination that pervades all social strata in China.' But in view of the heated arguments that had gone before, I deliberately rephrased and toned down this statement to read that there *appeared to be* discrimination. (Though the Chinese vehemently protested against the use of the word 'discrimination' at all, comrade Chen Yu—of the People's Congress—afterwards commended the euphemistic phrasing.) In my eight-point statement I charged that from our observation of instances, orders to discriminate against us appeared to have come from above rather than to have originated spontaneously from among the people. I told them we found it hard to reconcile the cases of apparently organised discrimination with the régime's declared policy of social equality. I asked to know whether by social equality they meant that Blacks are also equal to Whites and Yellows or whether their social equality excluded the Blacks. The plan was that after I had framed the charge, other students were to supply the evidence from their own several experiences.

Before narrating what happened next I shall have to digress again in order to give some idea of our general line of attack. The students never really had much opportunity of citing instances of discrimination because pandemonium broke loose just at the time when this evidence should have been presented.

Though white students were allowed to shop in the special stores originally meant for diplomatists and communist bosses only, African students were often refused the privilege. If African students were being debarred because they were students, then any other student, whatever his country or colour, should have been debarred also. But that was not the case—only Africans were disallowed. The situation in some hotels was the same as in the shops.

There are no 'Whites only' or 'Chinese only' or 'Blacks not allowed here' notices to be seen anywhere, but you may stand wondering why you are not allowed to enter this shop and then see your white college mate entering without molestation. That is as bad as 'Blacks not allowed', I think.

At the time before the Albanian students came to Peking, we Africans were in the majority in the Language Institute. There were then seven African nationalities and we mixed freely with Indonesians, Mongols, Russians, Koreans, Rumanians, Cambodians, Vietnamese, Burmese and Latin Americans; there was no overt race or colour consciousness. But when Khrushchev had his famous argument with Enver Hoxha and Albania attained to the very unenviable status of satellite to Red China, one hundred Albanians, mostly those sacked from Soviet universities, arrived in Peking to form the largest single foreign nationality in the Institute. It was not at all clear what those Albanians were so proud about, except it be that their country is definitely socialist and satellite to China. Our countries and parties, on the other hand, were only aspirants to a vague kind of socialism, which they are not even able to define to anybody's satisfaction. In these, and only these, terms, the Albanians were superior to us, and the Chinese did their best to connive at the discriminatory practices of the Albanians. Service in our refectory had previously been on the basis of first come first served, but after the Albanians arrived, it became White first, Black after. The story was the same in all cases where some sort of

priority had to be established. The Chinese failed to
deal with cases reported to them, fearing to displease the
Albanians. It has always been a glaring fault of the
Chinese that they over-indulge their political favourites,
thus establishing an arbitrary pecking order.

Whereas all other foreigners took 100 yuan a month
each, the Albanians took 150 yuan. This was another
sore point. There was nothing at all to warrant the
Albanians taking more than we. We ate the same food
in the same hall, and, if anything, dressed better than
they and therefore needed more money for clothing
(they all arrived in brown trousers and brown wind-
cheaters which appear to be their counterpart of the
Chinese eternal blue). What looked queer about the
whole business was that the Chinese had told the
Albanians not to let us Africans know that they (Albanians) were taking 150 yuan. It is quite possible to
argue that we were each being paid according to the
agreement with the respective home organisations. But
then, the agreement with our home organisations specified 80 yuan, which was increased to 100 yuan *without
consulting those home organisations*, after we had ourselves proved that it was not enough and asked for more.
If the Albanians needed 150 yuan to live comfortably, we
saw no reason why we should not do the same. This was
one of the ways in which the Chinese tacitly acknowledged
Albanian superiority over Africans, a privilege which the
Albanians used to the full, and mercilessly too. The
Chinese would do nothing to remedy the situation.

The Chinese have a term by which they addressed us:
Hēi rén, which literally translated means 'black man'.
The term as it stands is quite innocuous. When a professor
of anthropology mentions in his lecture the terms
'Semites', 'Hamites' and 'Negroes', neither he himself
nor his audience attach any emotional implication to these

terms. They remain names for human groupings with particular and definable morphological characteristics. But when a layman talks of 'negro' then the listener, particularly if he is himself a Negro, interprets the word, not according to its absolute scientific meaning, but according to the nature of the speaker and the place and circumstances under which it is spoken. In America the originally innocent race name 'Negro' has been twisted into a term of insult, sometimes modified into the more revolting term 'Nigger'. For that reason the moment I hear an American, or a white man, generally say, 'Negro', I think first and foremost of the insult, not of the scientific definition. On the other hand an American who has been a close crony and has never shown any sign of race consciousness in our relationship, can actually call me 'you black devil' or 'you Nigger' and make me accept these terms as endearing epithets. Person, place, circumstance and attitude—very particularly attitude—all count in the interpretation of such terms as have racial or tribal significance. What I argue is that the circumstances under and the attitude with which the Chinese term *Hēi rén* is used, all make 'Nigger' the only possible translation. I am not alone in thinking so either; all the other African students were of the same opinion. They found the term intensely offensive. (I refer you to Appendices I and II.) Our past experiences in colour discrimination have made us Africans over-sensitive on the subject, with the result that we are sometimes liable to misinterpret the attitudes and intentions of other races towards us. But I am satisfied, after relatively impassive observation and assessment, that our interpretation is correct.

To eradicate an evil like this in China is a very easy matter. The government need just publish one article on the subject in the *People's Daily* and that will be the end. There are no opposition papers to argue against it; no one to say that in the name of democracy he can call anybody any name he likes. But though we complained bitterly on sundry occasions, the authorities never once indicated that we had made any impression on them.

If the Chinese man-in-the-street thinks that your black skin is due to accumulated dirt, it is relatively easy to let someone persuade you that he does so in ignorance. But when a full-blooded doctor of medicine, whose science should have made him know better, asks you why your skin is still so black if you ever wash, it is difficult to believe that no insult is intended. Things like that did happen and the conclusion they led us to was that either the people (even the doctors) were supremely ignorant or supremely ill-intentioned. Doctors certainly cannot be supremely ignorant on matters of skin pigment. Such a question must certainly have sprung from malice, pure and simple.

Another form of discrimination practised against us was paternalism. The experts list it under discrimination though we laymen do not usually recognise it as such. In all their dealings with us the Chinese behaved as if they were dealing with people from whom normal intelligence could not be expected. Since paternalism draws or seeks to draw a dividing line between the superior attributes (real or imagined) of one person or group and the inferior attributes of another, it can be intensely offensive. We found Chinese paternalism particularly offensive because their superiority is more imaginary than real.

Yet another grievance of ours was that we had no social justice and security. We recognised it clearly through the Ali assault case. When the incident occurred the police did not take any statement from Ali, neither did they bother to question any of the foreigners who were on the spot and who, by the way, were unanimous

in their condemnation of Chinese brutality on that
occasion. What the police did was to take statements
from the Chinese side only and then give their 'judgment' on that. It is true that on a Wednesday evening
they came with intent to take Ali's statement, but they
brought along with them at the same time a written
and stamped 'judgment' pronouncing Ali guilty. We
found it difficult to understand this novel method of
administering justice: judgment first, statement afterwards. This case was establishing precedents, and if we
were to accept those precedents without question, it
would mean that any time there was an argument
between a Chinese and an African, any number of
Chinese could set upon the African and beat him up the
way they liked. After the beating the police would come
up with their 'judgment', in which the African would in-
variably be guilty. That was a vivid reminder of what
happens in apartheid South Africa and some colonial
régimes where magistrates are not expected to find a
white man guilty in a White versus Black legal suit.
Where then was our guarantee of social security? Where
was the guarantee that we would have equal justice?

Our last point was about the repeated attempt of the
Chinese to break up our Union. Quite apart from the
fact that we ourselves found it difficult to work together, our differences and difficulties were always
being increased by Chinese interference. We had more
important objects than seeking to win concessions from
the Chinese; the Union, properly managed, could have
been a valuable asset to both ourselves and the Chinese.
(Had we not just managed to nip one hunger strike in the
bud?) We wanted them to stop their game of weakening
and confusing us by pitting factions and nationalities
against each other.

These, in short, were the grievances for which we

sought redress. There was something else the Chinese were expecting but which was not in our minds at all at the time. They were expecting us to demand a rise in our monthly allowance; they were expecting us to demand the same 150 yuan that they were paying to the Albanians. In fact I believe this expectation of theirs was more responsible than anything else for the firm stand they took against us. As one of them (my old 'friend' Chen Yu) told me in private afterwards, they were extremely broke but could not tell us a thing like that in public. They had to bluff their way out by acting tough. (The matter of a rise in allowance was actually raised in our Central Committee meeting on March 11, 1962, but I and some others opposed it on grounds that in view of the peculiar conditions in China, we could not afford to turn our Union into an instrument for making demands. The matter could be taken up by individual nationalities if they saw fit, we concluded.)

To continue my narrative where I broke it off: the Chinese were seeing to it that the three they had got round to speak against us were having the most word. Abdallah spoke first and said that there was no racial discrimination in China and that such a thing was to be found only in South Africa and the United States and so on. Next, Muzong of Cameroun stood up to say that the Central Committee had never been authorised to speak for the Union and that they had no confidence in me, the Secretary-General and spokesman on that occasion. That brought me to my feet immediately. My authority had been seriously challenged; I had to have a vote of confidence before I could proceed. 'Stand up all those who recognise me as authorised spokesman of the union', I shouted. All the Zanzibari, Ghanaian and Camerounian students (except Nyobe and Muzong) stood up to give me their confidence vote. The Somali students still remained sitting because my speech had not yet been translated into Arabic. My move was a complete surprise to the Chinese, who frantically began to ask everyone to sit down, arguing that a confidence vote was not necessary. But I insisted. In the tumult the translation into Arabic could not be made. In spite of this it was already too clear that, even without the Somali votes, I already had the overwhelming majority on my side; had the voting been carried on to the end, only the three Chinese faithfuls, Nyobe, Muzong and Abdallah, would have given their votes to the Chinese. My friends advised me that it was no longer necessary to press for a confidence vote; so I let it go.

After quiet had been restored, Muzong was given the word again. He charged that our Union meetings had always been disorderly (there is some truth in this) and that the Central Committee were dictators. The fact of the matter is that, on one occasion when the Camerounian students were bickering at a Union meeting over issues not concerned with the Union but their own party, I put my foot down and ruled that no Camerounian could speak on that subject at our meetings. They should do it elsewhere. Muzong wanted to speak on this matter but was ruled out of order because the subject itself was out of order. He took this very ill and wrote to me expressing his grievance. The measure I took on that occasion was intended to curb that very disorderliness of which Muzong was now complaining in the presence of the Chinese.

The accusation of 'dictatorship' filled the cup to overflowing. A Camerounian student by name Talgu, who was sitting opposite Muzong, stood up and with no warning whatever of his intention, he proceeded to make his open palm collide with Muzong's mouth. The next thing we knew was Muzong sprawling on the ground. (The slap didn't look a powerful one, but Muzong happens to have very small, weak legs carrying a big head and trunk. His centre of gravity must have been in the wrong place.) In the confusion that followed someone else gave Abdallah a whack in the face which sent him cowering under the conference table.

My emotions upon seeing this display of violence were conflicting. I didn't know whether to sympathise with Muzong and Abdallah or whether to limit myself to saying: 'Serves 'em right, the traitors!' Those chaps (the Muzong bunch) had a perfect right to hold their own views and to disagree with us, but where their actions were motivated by no sublimer aim than to ingratiate themselves with the Chinese, we felt we had to draw the line somewhere, though not necessarily Talgu-style.

Condemn us? Perhaps, but you will likely be condemning yourself in the process. Why does Africa deny to Tshombe and his Katanga the right to choose the government under which they shall live, while supporting the East Africans' struggle for the break-up of their Federation? Is it not because we see in each of these a case of the foreigner versus the African? Tshombe is a willing instrument in the hands of foreigners who would partition the Congo and thus ensure for themselves the continuance of their unholy exploitation of Katanga's mineral wealth. Direct condemnation of Tshombe is at once an oblique condemnation of the foreigners who prod him. The East Africans we support because by breaking up the Federation, they weaken the power and influence of the white settlers who, because they refuse to realise and accept that it is they who must be absorbed into a black society and not the blacks into a white society, still qualify as foreigners in our land.

Now here was a bunch of three Africans who, for the

inglorious motive and dubious benefit of admission into
the Chinese Communist Party, would side with the
foreigner against Africans demanding an unconditional
end to racial discrimination. I must be plain nuts to
sympathise with the likes of them.

But one thing was clear: the violence displayed certainly should not have taken place, for we were at that very
time protesting against Chinese man-handling of some
of our number. Moreover, it appeared to lend a measure
of support to Muzong's charge that our meetings were
disorderly and that the Central Committee was dictatorial.
But that support is only apparent. In a body having four
official languages (English, French, Arabic and Somali),
into which all proceedings had to be translated (not
simultaneously), it is difficult not to expect some confusion, particularly as our interpreters were by no means
expert and no one could be really sure whether the interpretation had been done aright. The 'disorderliness'
which Muzong charged was often introduced by himself
and his other pro-Chinese comrades. We very often
debated issues for several consecutive meetings without
agreeing among ourselves. Were there a single person or
a small clique that could dictate to the rest, our business
would certainly have been dispatched more speedily,
as there would be no room for the opinions of others.
How does that tally with the charge of dictation? It is
noteworthy that despite heated arguments at our meetings, despite accusations and counter-accusations, no one
had ever resorted to either violently abusive language or
violent gestures. Again, had we planned that the
students should cause violence, we should have been the
first to insist that they should all take part in the conference from the very outset. But as it was, for three
whole hours we argued against their participation because
we feared that their mood might not permit of peaceful

discussion. The presence of the other students could have given the nine Committee members valuable moral support, but we were prepared to negotiate with twice our number of Chinese—give the Chinese all the advantage of numbers—just in order to prevent the upheavals we feared.

That Monday would have been the second day of the hunger and non-co-operation strike the students had demanded, if the Central Committee had not managed to avert the strike. In the tumult following the slappings it was we officers who calmed the students down and persuaded them to resume the talks. It was due to our efforts that those three traitors were not given a severe beating. In fact, had there been a Chinese at the Peace Hotel to act as sensibly and as collectedly as we of the Committee did that afternoon, Ali and that Zanzibari woman and her husband would not have been beaten up as mercilessly as they were. Do all these things argue against us or for us? In very fact, the Chinese tacitly admitted their fault in inviting the students and their own inability to control them by appealing to us to calm down the others, a task in which we did not fail. Yes, they appealed for help to that very Committee which, some hours before, they refused to recognise.

During the tumult the majority of the students walked out. They hadn't asked to attend the conference in the first place; they weren't prepared to stand any more nonsense from the Chinese, they said. But with great difficulty we managed to bring them back, and business resumed. Well, it is not quite correct to say 'business resumed', because when we sat down again we just flung hot words at each other across the conference table, each side trying to absolve itself from responsibility for the trouble. One Chinese woman, a high party member of the Women's Federation who had toured

G

Africa the previous year and should have known much better, went so far as to tell us that we should really accept the hated term *Hēi rén*—'Nigger'—as a compliment.

It must have been about an hour after the general disorder when five stalwart policemen marched into the conference room and arrested Talgu, the Camerounian student who slapped Muzong, and Tahir, a Zanzibari student who, the Chinese alleged, had shouted: 'Down with Chinese imperialism!' We calmly allowed the police to read out their charges, but when they tried to take the boys away we stood in their way and asked them to take us all along too. Angry though we were, there was no violence against the police, and no serious attempt to prevent them from performing their duty. But it was hard to accept that the Chinese should bring in the students against the students' own wish and our best advice and then start arresting them for the very thing we ourselves had done our best to prevent.

Even had there been time, the conference could not have continued. The Chinese had at long last agreed with us that the atmosphere at a conference really counts. They asked the other students to go home, leaving only the Committee to negotiate. Yes, they were now prepared to negotiate with the Committee they had refused to recognise. This vindicated the wisdom of our advice that the student-body need not have come. You could read the shame on their faces as they trooped out of the conference room, those bunglers. We turned down their suggestion.

Before the conference finally broke up at about 8 o'clock in the evening, a few more interesting things happened. Our Union President, Mr Kassim of Zanzibar, speaking for himself, cried fie on their non-existent Sino-African friendship and asked for his immediate repatriation. He wasn't prepared to continue associating with such shameless hypocrites. Kassim's demand was supported by another Zanzibari, a pretty girl called Rachman. In a fiery speech she told the Chinese, 'Send me back to Africa, Mother Africa!' You should have been in our shoes to understand what that meant to us. To this day I still remember Rachman as 'Mother Africa'.

I think I owe the Zanzibaris some justice since I have earlier spoken of them as 'playing good boys' to the Chinese. This was quite true of the seven who formed the first batch, but even they toed the Chinese line only in the beginning. As soon as they got to know the real character of the Chinese, they were as firm in their opposition as anyone else. On that fateful Monday, the Zanzibaris, particularly the girls—I recall the names of Zuena, Zulekha, Rachman and Mariam—showed more courage than any other single nationality.

After Rachman's impassioned speech, the sixteen remaining Zanzibaris joined in and asked for repatriation.

That night we slept in the conference room. We were not prepared to leave without our two friends who had been arrested. Singing, conversing and generally in high spirits, we waited through the night. Outside, light snow covered the roof tops. Inside, within each secret mind loomed the big question: What next?

At three in the morning, the ambassador of the Republic of Guinea and one of his *aides* came to see us. They had arrived about an hour earlier and had heard the details of the day's events from the Chinese. The two were later on joined by the *chargé d'affaires* of the Ghanaian embassy. The Guinean ambassador, I must stress, was a man of very good sense, a man who saw things in their right perspective and not just as the Chinese wanted him to see them. He was stern when the need arose and conciliatory at the right moment; so conciliatory at times that we were extremely embarrassed.

That gentleman won us over, but he didn't start by telling us how wrong we were in everything. He won our
hearts from the first by admitting that we had some
really serious grievances requiring investigation. He then
proceeded to point out where we went wrong and where
the Chinese went wrong. That man's logic was so perfect
and his arguments so impartial that we had to listen to
him. We did. For six whole hours, from three in the morning to nine o'clock, we listened to him and the Ghanaian
chargé d'affaires. It was at this time that the Guinean
ambassador told us the adage: 'It is comparison that disgraces the ass', but I was then translating his speech from
French into English and had no chance of asking him
exactly what he meant. The main request of the diplomatists was that we should go back to our colleges. When
we refused, pleading the non-return of the two friends
who were arrested, they promised to get the Chinese to
release them. They made good that promise.

The biscuits the Chinese had brought us for our supper
were still lying around because we refused to touch
them. We wouldn't eat them even on the advice of our
diplomatists, but we agreed to leave for our colleges in
obedience to them. This we did at nine o'clock on
Tuesday morning, March 27.

At about midday that Tuesday, our two arrested
friends, Talgu and Tahir, arrived back from detention.
(We promptly named them Prison Graduates in the best
nationalist tradition.) Eagerly we surrounded them to
learn what had happened while they were under detention. They related to us that they were locked in separate
cells after they had been thoroughly searched. Not long
after the lock-up, each person was taken before an
officer supposed to be a judge. That man was the same
police officer who had arrested them. He took no statement from them, he called no witnesses; he only asked

them to confess. If they would only confess they wouldn't be heavily punished; they might even go scot-free. This method of administering justice was so new to our friends that they did not know how to cope with it. They had nothing to confess except that Talgu did in fact slap Muzong and that Tahir never shouted the slogan 'Down with the Chinese imperialists', although he would have been perfectly right and correct if he had done so. Threats, pleadings and outright bribery all failed to extort the desired confession throughout the frequent interrogations to which they were subjected for the whole night. In the morning, the Guinean ambassador intervened and obtained their release as he had promised to do.

Thus ended Sino-African friendship so far as we were concerned. That diaphanous and intangible something called Sino-African friendship evaporated into thin air before our very eyes. Many Africans there may be who harbour really friendly feelings towards China, but for the Chinese no such thing as friendship towards the Africans exists. They know it pays them to make us feel they are our friends, and their hypocritical protestations of amity will continue till they get what they want from us. Then for the rest, we shall have only snarls.

Sino-African friendship, my foot!

15

The Aftermath

My story now draws to a close. It only remains to re-count the aftermath of the March disturbances. That very Tuesday, March 27, 1962, all the eighteen Zanzibari students handed in their passports to the dean and demanded their fare home. That same night, three of the four Zanzibaris working at Radio Peking also handed in their passports and started to pack for home. A week or so later, they received a cable from the Secretary-General of their party asking them to wait until he came to Peking before taking further action. They were still waiting for their Secretary-General to arrive when I left Peking on April 11.

Three days after the disturbances I also handed in my passport to the authorities of the Medical College. The Chinese were extremely alarmed. Twenty-two Africans leaving China at about the same time, and in anger: this was something they were very anxious to conceal from the world. They set about inviting us in small groups to meetings and parties. I attended three of these palavers.

During this period before my departure, I learned a few more useful lessons. I have explained elsewhere how in China even personal friendships are rigorously controlled by the Party. I got further and incontrovertible proof of this during my last fortnight. To enable you to understand, I have to begin at the beginning. In my

early days at the Medical College, I found that no
Chinese student or teacher would approach me. On
arriving I was taken to my room with never a word about
where to find what in the college. Perhaps you are
thinking I would have fared better if I had been more of a
go-getter. But in China you just don't go about things in
that way. Just mark this: there was a student from
Uganda called Okidi in Peking University. He had been
there for six months when I first met him. During this
period he had tried to find out from the Chinese students
how many faculties and of what sort there were in the
University. Nobody was ready to tell him. It is hardly
credible that the Chinese students didn't know what
faculties their own university had. But such things
appear to be top secrets in China. Nobody would tell
without specific authority to do so.

When I found the Chinese cold towards me, I was at
first neither surprised nor daunted. But when the cold-
ness continued for a month, I grew angry. My first
really hot argument in China was when one of our
interpreters waxed indignant at my suggestion of going
round to look at the Medical College *unaccompanied*. This
was unheard of talk, apparently, even coming from
someone who could not get anyone to perform the normal
courtesy of telling him where everything was.

So there was I at the Medical College not knowing the
first thing about the place, its layout, facilities and so on.
One day about a month after my arrival, I went down
with a severe cold. I didn't know where the college's
clinic was, and no one was willing to tell me. By then I
had come to realise there was a special reason, in addition
to the normal ones, why people held aloof from me and
were unhelpful. The first African student to be admitted
to the Medical College, a man from Uganda, went back
home leaving a bad record behind him. According to one

of his fellow countrymen, he had borrowed money from Chinese students and failed to pay it back. He had also failed to pay for some of the food supplied to him in his last days there. As soon as I learned of this man's unsavoury reputation, I felt it my duty to do all I could to correct the bad impression for my own sake and for the sake of all Africans studying in Peking, then and in the future. I don't think it's boasting to say I acquitted myself not uncreditably.

Suffering from a heavy cold and not knowing where the clinic was, I went up to the prefect of our class and put it squarely to him that he, his class, the staff and everyone else were punishing me for the offences of the scoundrelly Ugandan. They vehemently rebutted the charge, but I could see I had hit the mark. Accuse a Chinese of anything; if the accusation is wrong, he will dismiss it in a more or less level-headed way. But if the accusation is true, he will burst into loud and emphatic protestation. You can judge the truth or otherwise of your accusations by the nature of the Chinese reaction to them.

Well, that afternoon, I was shown to the clinic and in the evening a troop of classmates came in to visit me. They came under the leadership, of course, of the Party secretary of the class, and put on the widest ingratiating grins I have ever seen. After that, there was no more segregation and relations were tolerably cordial—until the day I announced my intention of leaving China. All those who had formerly pretended to be friends suddenly left me and scrupulously avoided me on all occasions. It was if I had caught overnight a highly infectious and obnoxious disease. When we encountered on the campus, they pretended I wasn't there, a striking contrast to their recent attitude to their lone African 'friend' in the college. Clearly, the Party can switch on and off people's love and hate at will.

That this 'sending to Coventry' wasn't a natural reaction is shown by the fact that one 'friend' did still stick to me like a leech. This was our form prefect. Every free moment of his time was spent in my room. He would stay with me until eleven o'clock at night, although by regulation all Chinese students had to be in their rooms by nine-thirty. I had already stopped attending lectures, so he wasn't there on the pretext of helping me in my studies. What he was trying to find out was the things I intended to say about China once I got out into the outside world. At times the hostile atmosphere was so strong that I began to wonder if indeed I should be allowed to leave China alive.

*   *   *

This is the China I saw and experienced: the China which so enchants many leading figures in African politics that they want to make it their model. They must be able to read deeper meanings into China's realities than my limitations will enable me to do. But I am not so limited and stupid that I cannot form a sound opinion of what is happening in China, and what the dangers are for Africa in the Chinese plan to convert the continent to communism.

Postscript

Communist imperialism is a stark reality that we in Africa ignore at our peril. We must understand that the communists, given the right opportunity, will deal out to us the same treatment as they now mete out to those once free nations which have fallen under their domination.

By 'imperialist', Africans usually mean all those European powers (Britain, France, Belgium, Spain and Portugal) which have at one time or another held colonies in Africa and in other parts of the world. The term is extended to include the United States. To call such countries 'imperialist' is just and proper. They have dominated, and still seek, some of them, to dominate, other weaker peoples either politically, economically or ideologically, or by a combination of these imperialistic methods. The essence of the imperialism practised by the 'imperialist powers' is the exploitation of the economic and human resources of dependent countries principally for the benefit of the exploiter.

How do the Soviet Union and China measure up when this test of imperialism is applied to them? Since the Second World War, the Soviet Union has managed to dominate ideologically, politically and economically, Poland, Czechoslovakia, Hungary, Rumania, East Germany, Bulgaria, Latvia, Lithuania and Estonia. These countries were certainly non-communist before the Nazi armies over-ran them. Soviet forces drive out the

Germans, and lo! these states turn communist almost overnight: they have remained so ever since.

But did they not welcome communism, you say? Do they not accept it as the system they most like? If this is so, how then do you account for the large numbers of desperate refugees who were fleeing daily from Eastern to Western Germany before the communists built 'the wall of shame' between the two halves of Berlin? The Emperor Chin of China built the Great Wall to keep his *enemies out*; the communists in Eastern Germany built their great wall to keep *their own citizens in*. If you were in paradise, and the communists claim their countries are paradises on earth, would you need a great wall or an electrified fence to keep you in paradise?

Communist China came into being as a power in the world barely thirteen years ago. Yet within this short space of time, she has managed to swallow Tibet, provoke border disputes and then enforce border settlements in her favour with Burma, Pakistan, Nepal, Afghanistan and Outer Mongolia; and she is now engaged in eating into Indian territory. Is there any country today which can beat the Chinese record of border disputes? China can only be compared with Nazi Germany; like the Nazis, the Chinese communists are searching their borders and adjacent territories with hungry eyes, looking for more and more *Lebensraum*.

Seeing all that China and Russia have done and are doing, am I still to believe that they will not get their claws into territory in Africa, if they have the chance? They make great play of the fact that they have no colonies in Africa. They weren't there when Africa was partitioned. But where they have been offered the chance elsewhere in the world, they have shown they can teach the traditional imperialist nations a thing or two when it comes to colonising and exploiting weaker peoples.

Since 1945, Britain has granted independence to
India, Burma, Ceylon, Ghana, Nigeria, Sierra Leone and
other former colonies and is completing the process of
further decolonisation in Africa and other parts of the
world. Within the same period France also has granted
political independence to her former colonies. Yes, you
may say, but great pressure was brought to bear on the
French and English. The rising tide of nationalism,
particularly in Africa, has made the old imperialism
impossible to maintain. This is true. But yet compare the
number of states which have achieved independence
from colonial rule with those who, since 1945, have dis-
appeared as free states to become communist colonies.
When the people in Ghana and Nigeria, for example,
protested against colonial rule, and made it clear they
were ready to fight for freedom, Britain realised that the
world was changing and that Africans were as much entitled to national independence as Englishmen. Ghana
and Nigeria became free. But when the people of Hungary and Tibet protested against foreign domination, did
Russia and China accept that the world was changing and
that weaker peoples were entitled to national independence as much as great nations? No. Like brutal
conquering powers of the past, they crushed Hun-
garians and Tibetans to the earth. And this they call
'liberation'!

The political imperialism of Britain and France is
either dead or fast dying. Portuguese and Spanish imperialists may cling on a little longer, but their doom is
sealed. It is true, as many African leaders have pointed
out, that many of the former colonisers will try to maintain an economic control over the peoples to whom they
have granted political independence. But to my mind it is
utter folly for our political leaders to concentrate all their
attention on combating the last dying efforts of Western

imperialism while remaining utterly oblivious to the other and newer danger threatening from the communist imperialists.

We must defend our continent against imperialists. But we need to bring our definition of 'imperialism' up-to-date. We have to realise that imperialists come in all colours: white, yellow and black; yes, even black.

The communists make no secret of their intention of converting the whole world to communism. Recent history shows that they are quite prepared to do the converting by force. But even more dangerous than direct subjugation, because less obvious, is conversion by gradual subversion.

A very important step in the conversion of Africa to communism is the training of African propagandists in the countries of the communist bloc. The communists very clearly realise the advantage of training Africans to do their work for them. The scholarships offered by them to African students are intended to recruit agents for communism. To that end, such students are exposed to systematic indoctrination and direct political instruction, whatever the course of formal studies. As I have pointed out, education at a communist university is wholly different from education in a Western-type university. African students studying in China, Russia and so on are exposed to such carefully planned and massive indoctrination and propaganda that only a few of the very strong-willed can have any hope of escaping unscathed.

The communist bloc will soon be flooding the African continent with thousands of young, energetic Africans, ready to believe that their own countries will be sending up sputniks and spacemen within a few years if only they adopt the communist system. Because Africa has as yet not developed an effective counter-balance to these pro-communist forces in her midst, there is very little resistance to them.

The communists assert that whatever they do for African countries is from purely disinterested motives, and that it is only the Western countries which attach strings to aid. So far they have been pretty successful in fooling us into believing this, because of the clever way they bait the hook. They conceal the hook so cleverly that you don't suspect its presence; you only see the very attractive bait. It is only after you have swallowed the bait that you discover to your dismay that there is something sticking in your throat. But by then it is too late: a hook is made to go in easily and never come out.

In some unguarded moments they slip up through being too hasty and greedy. Such a moment occurred when I was in Peking. A delegation from Ghana asked Chou En-lai for places in Chinese institutions of higher study. Chou was prepared to grant fifty places, but the Ghanaians pressed for more, for a hundred. Finally Chou agreed, but only on condition that the extra fifty came to study Marxism and communist tactics exclusively. Ghana accepted the offer, but, though the students provided for under this agreement should have reached China by the end of 1961, they had not turned up by the time I left Peking in April 1962.

But the fact is, the communists play their propaganda so well that the vast majority of people affected by it do not realise the aims behind their offering scholarships in communist countries to young Africans. And moreover the impression is created that it is only the communist countries which provide the benefits of higher education to Africans. This is partly due to the cleverness of communist propaganda, but also to the failure of the Western nations to take up the communist propaganda challenge.

By cleverly organised tours for visiting delegates, by subtle propaganda over the air, the communists build up a picture of a wonderful world which communism will give all people, especially those in poor and weak countries. And all the time they are operating an imperialist plan to gain control over all people.

I do not suggest that communist lies should be countered by yet more lies. What is needed is that lies should be countered by truth, and that adequate provision should be made to foil communist encroachments on our political, economic and ideological freedom.

When I was a small boy, my companions and I were in such a desperate hurry to grow big that we never tired of arguing who was taller. Whenever such an argument arose, we used to settle it in a very simple way: by standing back to back. A third playmate acted as arbiter, scrutinised the levels reached by the two small heads, and then gave an incontrovertible verdict.

Why all the involved, tortuous arguing about where the real paradise lies—in the West or in the East, under capitalism or under communism? Why this headlong rush towards mutual destruction just to prove the superiority of political ideologies? Those who are so certain sure of their own ideo-political superiority should not be averse from standing back to back with their opponents, rather than face to face and armed to the teeth.

Let every country open its doors, lift its curtains and raze its walls. If people are free to travel to any part of the world to see things for themselves; if people can freely read books, magazines and papers, no matter where they originate; if they can freely exchange ideas with men and women in other lands—what need we to argue about the superiority of ideologies? The common people, who should be the final arbiters in the argument, will have every chance to decide what is superior and what they think best for them.

It is only those who have something to hide, whose régimes and systems are something different from the impression given of them to the outside world by official propaganda, who need be afraid of standing back to back with other and rival systems, and of abiding by the freely considered verdict of the people of the world.

Appendices

APPENDIX I

GHANA TRADES UNION CONGRESS INTERNATIONAL DEPARTMENT

STANDING INSTRUCTIONS FOR STUDENTS ATTENDING CHINESE UNIVERSITIES

1 *Language*
It is the general principle that foreign students in China must study the Chinese language for a year. This is the medium of instruction in all Schools, Colleges and Universities.

2 *University Entry Regulations*
   a. Scholarship holders must have passed the School Certificate Examination or its equivalent.
   b. Must have a Certificate concerning the state of his or her health.
   c. The duration of all university courses in China is five years excluding years of Chinese language study.
   d. Chinese Universities do not award degrees as obtained in other Western countries. In contrast, University leavers are awarded diplomas after completion of the particular field of study. In

effect this is in consonance with the socialist
educational policy of China. The Universities ensure that the students are well trained and could
be compared favourably with those trained in
other Western Universities if not better.

3 *Fees*
Education in China is free and this facility will be
extended to those awarded the scholarships.

4 *Accommodation*
The students will be given free accommodation.

5 *Medical Attention*
This is free in China and the same facilities will be
accorded our students.

6 *Stipends*
Each of the students will be given 80 yuan which is
equivalent to £G11. This money should be used as
pocket money in purchasing clothing, books and meals.
Normally Chinese students use at most 20 yuan a month.

7 *Passages*
Air passages will be booked for the students who are to
study in China. This means the means of transport from
Accra to China and back is free. Students who do not
want to finish their courses for obvious reasons and would
like to return home would have to pay their own fare to
Ghana.

AUTHOR'S COMMENTS

The Ghana Trades Union Congress gave us each a copy
of these instructions and told us it was an agreement we
were required to sign before proceeding to China. In the
light of my later knowledge, I can say that these instructions came direct from the Chinese government

through their embassy in Ghana. Zanzibari students on their way to China were detained in Cairo for a month until they had signed a similar document.

With regard to the information about medical fees: I paid from my own pocket for medical services in the Union Hospital and in another hospital in Peking. The Language Institute regularly paid for treatment given us in the Third Medical Hospital, attached to Peking Medical College. A story in my language textbook taught us in very clear terms that 'consultation' was free, but 'treatment' was charged for.

As regards the stipend: my monthly expense account in Peking would run something like this:

	yuan
Food	50
Smokes and drinks ..	12
Laundry	5
Transport	5
Books and stationery ..	5
Soap and toilet goods	10
Union subscriptions ..	0.5

We spent little on books in the Language Institute, but in my first month at the Medical College I spent about 100 yuan (money coming from Ghana) on books. To prepare for the hard winter of 1961–2 I spent nearly 200 yuan of money from home on clothing.

APPENDIX II

ZANZIBARI STUDENTS' STANDPOINT

On behalf of Zanzibari students I have been authorised to say the following:

1 For a long time the students from various African countries have been complaining about the social life of China. Some have even returned home before the completion of their courses. Different nationalities have gone respectively to discuss the matter with the School Authority, but nothing so far has been gained. Now we realise that through unity we may solve these problems. So, Comrades, let us unite and let us hope for a solution to our problems.

2 *Problems*
To sum up the problems we are facing:
   (i) We Africans are not allowed to make friends of both sexes here in Peking. The Chinese authorities' excuse has been that they do not allow prostitution in China. This is rather strange. It is only when Chinese mix with Africans that there is fear of prostitution. Foreigners, other than Africans, are allowed freely to mix with Chinese—there is no fear of prostitution. Do the Chinese authorities mean to say that there is prostitution in other socialist countries where Africans mix freely with both sexes? We have so many cases showing how Chinese friends have been severely punished for the sole crime of mixing with Africans.
   (ii) We Africans are looked down upon; we are regarded more as animals than as human beings. It is a *crime* for Africans to enter some hotels and

some shops here in Peking. In dancing halls Africans are strictly observed and later our partners are thoroughly questioned. This is the so-called 'indestructible friendship' between Chinese and Africans.

(iii) Whenever we have complaints the Chinese authorities neglect them until *threatened*. This shows they are not at all concerned about our problems, but about the consequences resulting therefrom.

3 *Misinterpretation*

Rumours have been spread by the Chinese authorities that the African students have been induced by a third party * to make trouble. This act of shame by the Chinese authorities is aimed at destroying the Union. Cocktail parties have been arranged by the Chinese authorities inviting various groups of African nationalities. Every measure has been taken by the Chinese authorities not only to split the Union, but, and which is worse, to create misunderstanding, hatred and distrust among the African students themselves.

Zanzibari students know that there is no force on earth that can split African students' unity. The Chinese authorities thought they could do this, but the result is that African students have never been so closely united as they are today.

4 *Our standpoint*

In protest against the above, we propose the following measures:

(i) *Not* to attend class and to boycott all school activities for a week starting instantly after the meeting today, March 25, 1962.

* Mr John Holmes, who protested to the authorities over their handling of the Ali affair.

(ii) *Not* to eat within the said week.
(iii) During this period all should be done through the Central Committee of the African Students' Union to express our indignation to the Chinese authorities.
(iv) Should the Chinese authorities fail to comply with our demands, we should not be blamed for the consequences resulting therefrom.

5 *Warning*

In this meeting majority decision is *Final*. If at all there are some members who would not agree to some resolutions, they have to follow and observe what has been passed, or else in our opinion the persons concerned should be dismissed from the African Students' Union. We shall regard those persons as the greatest enemies of African Unity.

We Trust In You
Fellow Africans

Long Live African Unity!
Down With All Enemies Of Africa!

Secretary-General
Zanzibari Students' Union.

APPENDIX III

RESOLUTION OF THE CAMEROUNIAN STUDENTS

Notre point de vue sur la vie des étudiants africains en Chine

1 Recueillons de tous les Africains, étudiants en Chine, tous renseignements ayant trait à leur vie quotidienne et au comportement des camarades chinois vis-à-vis des étudiants africains, et ayant trait au comportement des étudiants africains vis-à-vis des camarades chinois, pouvant compromettre l'amitié sino-africaine.

Voir détail de ce comportement ici à l'Institut (cuisine, buvette etc.) et en ville.

2 Le problème des relations sociales entre chinois et étudiants africains:

    (a) isolement des étudiants africains par les camarades chinois;

    (b) arrestation des filles chinoises pour le seul fait qu'elles sont en relation avec nous;

    (c) haine aux étudiants africains: voyons le cas du camarade Aly, battu presqu'à mort à l'hôtel de Paix, et d'une femme africaine battue également à la même place et au même heure par plusieurs chinois devant les agents de sécurité sans intervention de ces derniers;

    (d) considérons également le fait que les deux victimes africains ci-dessus cités n'ont reçu aucun soin de sauvetage du potentiel humain qu'après 8 heures de temps;

    (e) la passivité des autorités de l'Institut pour sauver la vie à un étudiant qui est à leur contrôle direct en Chine.

3 Résumé de tous cela: pas de fraternité entre étudiants africains et camarades chinois.

4 En un bloc: nous reconnaissons la contribution du peuple chinois au movement de libération raciale dans le monde et au renversement de l'impérialisme. Mais en tant qu'étudiants africains, en Chine pour la réalisation de la cause commune du prolétariat selon le grand appel de Karl Marx: 'Prolétaires de tous les pays, unissez-vous!', nous nous sommes indignés devant l'acte survenu à la femme d'un ouvrier africain en Chine.

5 En bloc, nous inscrivons sur notre drapeau de revendications estudiantines les relations sociales normales entre la jeunesse chinoise et la jeunesse africaine, sans ce qu'on s'expose à l'accusation de discrimination raciale.

6 Le bilan des éléments qui constitue le corps de nos revendications sera présenté par écrit directement au Comité Central du Parti Communiste Chinois par les délégués de l'Union, et tous les autres compléments seront verbaux.

TRANSLATION

Our views about the life of African students in China

1 We record all the information gathered from African students in China regarding their daily life and regarding such attitudes of Chinese comrades towards African students, and of African students towards Chinese comrades, as could compromise Sino-African friendship.

    We refer to such attitudes as are manifested here in the Institute (in the kitchen, refectory, etc.) and in the town.

2 The problem of social relations between African students and Chinese:

    (a) ostracism of African students by Chinese comrades;

    (b) arrest of Chinese girls for the sole reason that they have relations with us;

    (c) ill-will towards African students: here we cite the case of comrade Ali who was beaten almost to death at the Peace Hotel, and of the African woman who was also beaten nearly to death at the same place and time, while several policemen stood by and made no move to intervene;

    (d) we take into consideration also the fact that the two African victims referred to above did not receive any first-aid till eight hours after the event;

    (e) the inaction displayed by the authorities at the Institute when it was a question of saving the life of a student placed under their direct charge in China.

3 In short, there is no spirit of brotherhood between African students and Chinese comrades.

4 In general, we recognise the contribution of the Chinese people to the world movement for racial liberation and for the overthrow of imperialism. But as African students in China in order to fulfil the common cause of the proletariat in accordance with the great appeal of Karl Marx: 'Workers of the world, unite!', we are indignant at the act perpetrated against the wife of an African worker in China.

5 We include in our list of demands the establishment of normal social relations between Chinese and African young people, without which there is danger of an accusation of racial discrimination.

6 The list of our grievances shall be presented in writing directly to the Central Committee of the Chinese Communist Party by the delegates of this Union, and all further details shall be verbal.